2008 CODING WORKBOOK for the Physician's Office

Alice Covell, CMA-A, RMA, CPC

DELMAR
CENGAGE Learning™

Australia • Brazil • Japan • Korea • Mexico • Singapore • Spain • United Kingdom • United States

DELMAR
CENGAGE Learning™

2008 Coding Workbook for the Physician's Office
Alice Covell

Vice President, Career and Professional Editorial: Dave Garza

Director of Learning Solutions: Matthew Kane

Senior Acquisitions Editor: Rhonda Dearborn

Managing Editor: Marah Bellegarde

Product Manager: Jadin Babin-Kavanaugh

Vice President, Career and Professional Marketing: Jennifer McAvey

Marketing Director: Wendy Mapstone

Executive Marketing Manager: Lynn Henn

Marketing Coordinator: Chelsey Iaquinta

Production Director: Carolyn Miller

Production Manager: Andrew Crouth

Senior Content Project Manager: James Zayicek

Senior Art Director: Jack Pendleton

ISBN-13: 978-1-4354-2595-8
ISBN-10: 1-4354-2595-2

Delmar Cengage Learning
5 Maxwell Drive
Clifton Park, NY 12065-2919
USA

Cengage Learning products are represented in Canada by Nelson Education, Ltd.

For your lifelong learning solutions, visit
delmar.cengage.com

Visit our corporate website at **www.cengage.com**

Printed in United States of America
1 2 3 4 5 XX 10 09 08

Contents

How to use the Encoder Pro 30-Day Free Trial CD-ROM

The Encoder Pro software included in the back cover of this textbook is presented as a 30-day free trial of Ingenix's powerful medical coding solution that allows you to look up ICD-9-CM, CPT, and HCPCS Level II codes quickly and accurately. This software can be used to assign codes to any exercise in the textbook. Be sure to check with your instructor before installing the Encoder Pro software because the CD-ROM bundled with your book expires 30 days after installation.

Menus and Toolbars

Encoder Pro contains a menu that expands to allow you to easily navigate the software. Click on a menu heading to select one of its options, such as View, Code Book Sections, etc. Encoder Pro contains a toolbar with drop-down menus that allow you to select the ICD-9-CM, CPT, or HCPCS Level II coding system and new/revised/deleted codes and code book sections.

- Use the coding system drop-down menu on the far left to select a coding system. Then, enter a condition (e.g., diabetes) or procedure/service in the Search box. Click the Search button to view Tabular Results, which can be expanded, or click the "See index listing" to use the alphabetic index to locate a code.
- Use the drop-down list on the far right of the black toolbar to quickly access New Codes, Revised Codes, Deleted Codes, and Code Book Sections. Make a selection and click the View button to access the dialog boxes.
- Encoder Pro's toolbar with clickable buttons allows you to use its unique features. Simply mouse over a button to view its title, and a brief description of the button will also appear in the status bar on the bottom left of the screen. Click on the button to use its function.

Features and Benefits of Encoder Pro

Encoder Pro is the essential code lookup software for CPT®, ICD-9-CM, and HCPCS code sets. It gives users fast searching capabilities across all code sets. Encoder Pro can greatly reduce the time it takes to build or review a claim, and helps improve overall coding accuracy. If you decide to subscribe to the full version of Encoder Pro, the following tools will be available to you:

- **Powerful Ingenix CodeLogic™ search engine.** Improve productivity by eliminating time-consuming code lookup in outdated code books. Search all three code sets simultaneously using lay terms, acronyms, abbreviations, and even misspelled words.
- **Lay descriptions for thousands of CPT® codes.** Enhance your understanding of procedures with easy-to-understand descriptions.
- **Color-coded edits.** Understand whether a code carries an age or sex edit, is covered by Medicare, or contains bundled procedures.

- **Quarterly update service.** Rest assured you are always using accurate codes. You can code confidently throughout the year with free code updates.
- **Great value.** Get the content from over 20 code and reference books in one powerful solution.

For more information about Encoder Pro software, click on the Help menu from inside the free trial version, then select "Features by Product," or go to www.ingenixonline.com.

Preface

Many billers learn to code on their own, by trial and error. They open the books, search for a code, and take the first one that looks correct. If they use an inaccurate code on a medical claim form, the payer may reject or pay incorrectly for that service. Insurance companies monitor the reported procedures and diagnoses, looking for fraud or abuse. Medicare, the Blues, managed care plans, and other payers issue utilization reports advising physicians that their reported services differ from those of their peers. These reports can be the precursor for audit by that payer. These are money matters, but coding can impact medical issues. Disease registries state that patients are enrolled for care with an erroneous diagnosis. As a result, the doctor receives information on treatment of the wrong medical condition.

With so much of medicine and patient care decided by these codes, why is it so difficult to get them right? Most physicians do not speak code, at least not fluently. The terms in the coding references are concise, developed by a committee that carefully chooses which words to use. Busy doctors and other professionals describe their services in their own way. This becomes a bigger problem when English is the doctor's second language. Also, there are changes in procedure and diagnosis codes every year. Many office documents and computer systems contain obsolete codes.

Hospitals code differently than medical offices. Facilities may use CPT® for coding some outpatient services, but hospitals do not perform medical visits or surgery. Those are physician services. Unlike hospitals, insurers pay doctors on a fee for service basis. The doctor performs a service, bills it, and the payer sends a check. Both hospitals and doctors use the same diagnosis reference, ICD-9-CM, but the doctor's office may be limited to reporting only one code, the "best" one for the service. The U.S. Department of Health and Human Services (DHHS) developed official guidelines for coding diagnoses. Most of the guidelines apply to hospital reporting. Only sixteen rules specify diagnosis reporting by physicians. These instructions for physician coding appear later in this workbook.

Now that you have had the bad news, here is the good news. None of the coding process is secret. There are no hidden rules in obscure volumes. To master coding, all you do is read and think. Coding is logical, and it can be fun. So settle down with your coding references and this workbook, and enjoy.

Alice Covell, CMA-A, RMA, CPC

January 2008

Coding and Medical Insurance Policies

Coding can be significant in receiving, and keeping, payment for medical services. One publication says that coding makes a 25% greater or lesser difference in payment. It is the insurance policy language that defines payable benefits. Beginning coders may ask, "What code do I use to get paid?" A patient, not receiving payment, may say that the doctor reported the "wrong" code. The answer for both situations is clear. You always use the correct code.

Doctors find coding confusing. They may do a new service that does not have a specific code. Do we report it with an existing code number? Sometimes the procedure is not really new, but the doctor uses a new technique or technology. Medicare, the Blues, or another payer may notify the doctors to report these services under another code. However, without specific instructions to call the service something different, you should report it under the "unlisted procedure" code. The "Instructions for Use of the CPT Book" emphasize this point by stating, "Do not select a CPT code that merely approximates the service provided. If no such procedure or service exists, then report the service using the appropriate unlisted procedure or service code." The insurer can decide to pay or reject the claim, based on the policy coverage.

Perhaps a new code is now available for a recently developed procedure. Unfortunately, the service may be too new to appear on the insurance policy benefit list and so the payer rejects the claim. The doctor now wonders if you should code it with last year's code. You may decide to make the change after offering explanations to the irate patient who now has a large, unexpected bill. In these no-win situations, it may seem easier to recode and rebill the service. Don't do it. Resist that temptation. The medical record does not support any code but the correct one.

Insurers match the claims with their benefit schedule. Medicare pays for only a few preventive services. Religious organizations may have policies that do not cover sterilizations or abortions. Payers then send the doctor or policyholder the specified payment or a rejection. If you change the code to make the service payable, it is fraud. Also, a service may not be payable for the given diagnosis. Suppose the doctor sees a patient for bronchitis and notices that it is time to repeat the electrocardiogram, as the patient has a family history of heart disease. If the office bills the ECG with the diagnosis of bronchitis, the payer probably will reject the service. Taking an ECG is not a standard procedure for bronchitis. It is correct to report the office visit for bronchitis and the family history of heart disease for the ECG.

Some situations are less clear. No insurer would deny a person the reconstruction of his nose following a serious auto accident, a fall from a horse, or similar incident. What if the injury occurred ten years ago? Should the auto insurer, the owner of the stable, or the patient's own insurance pay the doctor's bill? Is the patient's health insurance primary, and expected to pay first before the other insurers? All these health insurance payment problems do not affect the determination of the correct diagnosis and procedure codes.

Medicare and private insurance are separate programs. Medicare's coding rules work, and the Health Insurance Portability and Accountability Act (HIPAA) requires insurers to adopt the government approved coding specifications of Medicare and Medicaid. If you work for a pediatrician, becoming aware of Medicare rules may be difficult. Pay close attention to payer bulletins and the information on coding distributed at their seminars and workshops. Many private organizations and medical specialty societies offer coding workshops. Try to attend one each year, and always end the year with the purchase of new coding references.

Conquering Coding

You may be surprised how much experience you have with coding. You use it every day. From social security, telephone, and credit card numbers, to thermometers and cable television selectors, numbers that represent words surround us. If you see $1.00, you think "one dollar." Even without a description or explanation, you probably recognize 1-800-555-1212.

Our present diagnosis coding system is ICD-9-CM, the International Classification of Diseases, Ninth Revision, Clinical Modification. Disease coding systems began in the late 1800s and identified the causes of death. The ICD system is now used worldwide to record the incidence of disease. Many ICD-9-CM reference books include this history. Take the time to read this fascinating summary of disease recording. ICD-9-CM is a three-volume reference, available from many sources at prices ranging from $19.95 to almost $200.00.

The American Medical Association (AMA) developed the procedure, or service coding reference, *Current Procedural Terminology,* or *CPT*®. This single volume reference is available from many sources, but the AMA carefully protects the copyright and printing of CPT.

The Health Care Financing Administration (HCFA), now named the Centers for Medicare and Medicaid Services (CMS), the agency responsible for Medicare and Medicaid, recognized that many medical services were not physician services. To report, pay, and monitor ambulance services, medical equipment, and supplies, another set of codes was needed. This system is called the Healthcare Common Procedure Coding System, or HCPCS (pronounced "hick-picks"). HCPCS has two levels of codes, usually indicated by Roman numerals. The Level I codes are the CPT codes, five digit, all numeric codes. Level II codes have a letter followed by four numbers. The Level III codes, or "local" codes, were eliminated with the implementation of the HIPAA standardized code sets in October 2003.

Coding determines the appropriateness of treatment and the medical necessity for a service. Insurers compile statistics on the frequency of a service, sometimes identifying "abused" procedures. They state that many doctors do C-sections for their own convenience rather than patient need, for example. Monitoring the codes billed, Michigan Blue Shield found a physician who did almost half the endoscopic procedures reported in one year. A Medicaid program discovered a doctor who reported over 400 house calls in one day. The payers, like you, found these data unbelievable, audited the physicians, and recovered the overpayments.

Coding Ground Rules

I. Keep your coding references current. Purchase new books each year.

II. Know the coding rules and apply them properly.

III. Code only what the documentation supports.

IV. Match the diagnosis code with the procedure code. They must be "reasonable."

V. Review and update all charge tickets, computer files, and encounter forms annually.

INTRODUCTION TO *CURRENT PROCEDURAL TERMINOLOGY (CPT)*

The American Medical Association (AMA) released the first edition of *Current Procedural Terminology (CPT)* in 1966. It was similar to a coding system developed ten years earlier by the California Medical Association (CMA) called the California Relative Value System (CRVS). These codes were based on a four-digit system. In 1970, the AMA released the Second Edition of CPT, adding a fifth digit to make services more specific. The Third Edition was printed in 1973, and the Fourth Edition in 1977. Also, during this time, many insurance companies developed their own coding systems. Some payers used these coding systems internally and others required the doctor use these special codes to report services to that insurer.

By 1983, a government study identified over 120 different procedure-coding systems. It was impossible to match services in all these different coding systems, so the government mandated a standard coding system for Medicare and Medicaid. Beginning in 1984, the government required physicians to report all services in HCPCS for all Medicare and Medicaid claims. Also in 1984, the AMA modified the name of CPT and began including the year in the title.

CPT-1992 changed all the "visit" services, such as office calls, hospital care, and nursing home visits, to "evaluation and management" services. In spite of many articles in medical publications, seminars, and newsletters, some physicians still have trouble determining the exact level of care to use for a patient. While deciding the correct level of service is the responsibility of the physician, not the medical assistant or biller, we will explore these codes in the worksheets. Medicare required this change as part of their implementation of the Resource Based Relative Value Scale (RBRVS) mandated by Congress to reform the Medicare payment structure.

The present edition of CPT contains over 7,500 different descriptions of services. The AMA protects these codes and descriptions by a copyright. Look at the introductory pages of the current edition. They give credit to the CPT Panel and Advisory Committees responsible for developing these codes. The Table of Contents shows the organization of the references. Note that the largest section, as you would expect, is the Surgery listing. Appendix B summarizes the code changes since the last edition. This list identifies the codes you must update in your computer or on office documents. Some CPT vendors and the AMA have editions with color-coded pages, color keys, and thumb indexed pages to make it easier to use. Their terminology and illustration sections can provide guidance with unfamiliar terms. The CPT Index is not complete, but it can help you search for new codes.

Most successful projects start at the beginning. Look at the CPT Introduction. Many of the higher numbered codes, the E/M (evaluation and management) services, appear first since most physicians do these services. Any doctor can report a code from any section, if that is the service performed. However, reasonableness must be tested. Would a podiatrist perform neurosurgery? Not likely, but it could appear that way if you transpose digits in the procedure code. Later, we will work with a worksheet that looks at reasonable code matching. The terminology format, with the stem of the procedure before the semicolon, saves space and makes the page easier to read. This code layout is standard in the CPT, HCPCS, and ICD-9-CM references.

Coding guidelines appear in each CPT section. You must read these carefully to select the correct codes in this workbook. Procedure descriptions may be misleading if you have not read the rules. We will review the "separate procedures" in the surgery section. The "modifiers" do just that, they modify or change a service. They are so important that all modifiers are listed in CPT Appendix A. Complete your reading of the Introduction and review any terminology and anatomy pages. Now you are ready to start the worksheets.

Evaluation and Management Services

The first three worksheets cover the basic medical visit services provided by almost every health care professional. These are the Evaluation and Management (E/M) codes. The service descriptions are complete, but confusing. An understanding of terms is critical to accurate interpretation of the services. You must read the CPT definitions of commonly used terms carefully. If you are responsible for billing and have obsolete codes or descriptions on the office encounter forms, change them immediately. You may find an old code or modifier in your computer system. Delete them only after making certain you do not need them for statistical use. Contact the vendor of your computer system or software to find the correct procedure for handling obsolete codes and modifiers.

There are three to five levels of many E/M codes. Encounter forms may have a cell labeled "New Patient" and code 99201 listed with the description "Level 1." The guidelines also advise you that the descriptions vary for all Level 1 codes. As you review the instructions, look at the codes used for illustration. The presenting problems, time, and face-to-face clarifications are essential components of the service descriptions. Review the instructions on selecting a level of E/M service with the doctors and other professionals so that the documentation in the patient's medical record matches the service level reported.

CPT Appendix C provides some clinical examples for each level of service. These are identified by specialty and may help you select the correct code. Do not read anything into the case study that is not there. If we assumed that the patient was blind, obese, or had another complicating problem, the level of service might change. Base your interpretation on the information provided, and nothing else.

Remember our earlier reference to policy benefits deciding whether a code would result in payment? The same rules affect modifiers. Medicare allows the modifier -21, prolonged E/M service, when applied to only the high level codes. Other payers may not honor or may have special rules for using a specific modifier.

Following the guidelines section, CPT begins with the E/M codes. You will find explanatory information throughout the section. You must read these instructions. Many worksheet items use this additional material. The reformatted visit codes on the next page show the similarities and contrasts for these services. Some criteria are consistent for most codes. New patient services require all three key components, history, examination, and medical decision making. Established patient services need two of the three key components. The wording of the paragraph on counseling and coordination of care is consistent throughout the E/M codes.

This section, the visit codes, may be the most complex in CPT. From here it will become easier. Again, review the guidelines and other instructions carefully, as they explain the components of each code. Code the worksheets of E/M encounters, described in terms used by physicians, not the CPT committee. You may not agree with the level of the code listed on the answer sheet, but your choice should be from the same group of codes. Aren't we glad that choosing the appropriate level of E/M codes is the responsibility of the doctor and not the coders?

In 1995, the AMA and HCFA released the documentation standards for E/M services. These described the components of the medical history and the number of body areas and organ systems that the doctor must examine and document for each level of service. In 1997, HCFA clarified this list by identifying the mandatory elements of the exam. The doctor supports a detailed exam (99203) by documenting twelve to seventeen exam items. The complexity of medical decision making is also explained. Be certain there is a copy of these criteria in your office so anyone creating medical records can follow these guidelines. All payers should accept this documentation standard, and the AMA may include it in future editions of CPT.

When the first three E/M services are placed next to each other, it is easier to see the similarities and differences between the codes:

New Patient - 99201	**New Patient - 99202**	**New Patient - 99203**
Office or other outpatient visit for the evaluation and management of a new patient, which requires these three key components:	Office or other outpatient visit for the evaluation and management of a new patient, which requires these three key components:	Office or other outpatient visit for the evaluation and management of a new patient, which requires these three key components:
• a problem focused history;	• an expanded problem focused history;	• a detailed history;
• a problem focused examination; and	• an expanded problem focused examination; and	• a detailed examination; and
• straightforward medical decision making.	• straightforward medical decision making.	• medical decision making of low complexity.
Counseling and/or coordination of care with other providers or agencies are provided consistent with the nature of the problem(s) and the patient's and/or family's needs.	Counseling and/or coordination of care with other providers or agencies are provided consistent with the nature of the problem(s) and the patient's and/or family's needs.	Counseling and/or coordination of care with other providers or agencies are provided consistent with the nature of the problem(s) and the patient's and/or family's needs.
Usually, the presenting problem(s) are self limited or minor. Physicians typically spend 10 minutes face-to-face with the patient and/or family.	Usually, the presenting problem(s) are of low to moderate severity. Physicians typically spend 20 minutes face-to-face with the patient and/or family.	Usually, the presenting problem(s) are of moderate severity. Physicians typically spend 30 minutes face-to-face with the patient and/or family.

Name ______________________

Evaluation and Management – I (99201-99239)

2008 CPT Codes

These codes cover office visits, hospital daily visits, and medical services for patients in hospital observation units. Most physicians use visit codes, and sometimes they make up over 90% of the services performed by that doctor.

Remember, some E/M services may require modifiers.

1. Discussion of medications with patient's family, just before patient left the observation unit 99217
2. Hospital visit, will discharge patient tomorrow 99231
3. First visit, multiple complaints, meds for diabetes, arthritis, and hypertension reviewed and changed, as patient has rash secondary to present combination, also fulgurated wart on left ring finger 99204
4. Visit with nurse for diabetes education 99210
5. Six-month follow-up visit for patient # 3 above 99213
6. First day in observation unit, patient collapsed at shopping mall and continues to have an irregular heartbeat 99219
7. Admission to hospital for Boy Scout with severe poison ivy 99221
8. Initial office visit for child with chicken pox 99201
9. Eight-year-old girl seen again for severe sore throat and fatigue 99212
10. Admission to ICU for 72 y/o male with massive cerebral hemorrhage, respiratory failure, and coma 99223
11. Hospital visit for patient with severe reaction (rash, vomiting) to x-ray study dye, medication prescribed 99233
12. Comprehensive follow-up counseling visit, emotionally upset over child's behavior and marital problems, 3:15 to 4:00 p.m. 99215
13. Forty-eight-year-old male admitted to hospital for chest pain and discharged the same day when all diagnostic studies were within normal limits 99236

Name ______________________

Evaluation and Management – II (99241-99300)

2008 CPT Codes

Consultations occur when one physician or provider requests the OPINION of another physician or provider. The consultant may perform tests to establish the opinion or may initiate treatment. This term is sometimes misused, as when the "patient consults with the doctor." If the second physician assumes part or all the care of the patient, it is a referral and not a consultation. A surgeon is usually not a consultant, but is expected to take care of the patient's problem. Consultation codes have two subcategories: office/outpatient and inpatient. There are also codes for Emergency, Pediatric Critical Care and Transport, Critical Care, and Neonatal or Pediatric Critical Care Services.

1. Office consult for high school senior with a knee injury occurring during the homecoming game ____________
2. Extended follow-up visit NICU, unstable 2-month-old infant ____________
3. Initial hospital consult for male diabetic, back surgery 3 days ago, now has a severe urinary tract infection, emergency procedure scheduled for this afternoon ____________
4. One hr. in ER with 3-year-old attacked by pit bull, found unconscious with bruises and scrapes, no suturing required ____________
5. Admission of premature newborn to NICU ____________
6. Brief inpatient consult to rule out abscessed tooth in post-delivery female ____________
7. ICU consult for elderly female with cardiac arrest during gallbladder surgery, now in a coma ____________
8. Office consult for teenager with severe acne ____________
9. Injured 18-month-old infant transported to Children's Hospital, pediatrician in attendance for trip of 55 minutes ____________
10. Constant attendance, 1.5 hours critical care in ICU, 15-year-old male, comatose after diving accident ____________
11. Office consult for 80-year-old with Alzheimer's and previous stroke, now combative and incontinent ____________
12. NICU visit, five-day-old infant, now weighing 4200 grams, will transfer to nursery tomorrow ____________
13. Seen again in observation unit, comprehensive history/exam, will transfer to surgeon if not improved in 24 hours ____________

Name ____________________

Evaluation and Management – III (99304-99499)

2008 CPT Codes

These codes are used to report Nursing Facility and Rest Home care, Home Services, and Miscellaneous care. They cover special or preventive services that may be exclusions under some insurance policies. Be certain the codes you report accurately reflect the services performed so the insurer can appropriately pay or reject the claim. Some services may be payable only for certain diagnoses or in specified locations.

1. Follow-up house call for child recovering from flu ____________
2. Comprehensive admission services for the transfer of a psychotic patient from an acute care hospital to psychiatric residential treatment center ____________
3. Annual nursing facility visit ____________
4. Visit to a home for the developmentally disabled to see a new patient with recent onset of swelling in hands and feet ____________
5. One hour conference at day-care center with family and geriatric assessment staff, pending transfer of patient ____________
6. Forty-five minute conversation over three days with an established patient threatening suicide ____________
7. Initial exam of infant born at home ____________
8. One-hour discussion with family of elderly patient now discharged from rehabilitation facility to son's home for aftercare ____________
9. New patient, annual exam, pilot, age 47 ____________
10. Follow-up visit to foster care home for Alzheimer's patient with urinary tract infection ____________
11. Standby services (25 minutes) required for cesarean/high risk delivery ____________
12. Counseling on risk factors, sexually active 14-year-old female, forty-five minutes ____________
13. Preschool exam for 5-year-old seen since infancy ____________
14. Services for June (25 minutes) supervising the hospice team for care of terminally ill cancer patient. Patient not seen. ____________
15. Initial home visit to discuss care options with family of 88-year-old disabled stroke patient, 1 hour ____________

Name ______________________

Anesthesia Services (00100 – 01999)

2008 CPT Codes

Physicians who are not anesthesiologists may report anesthesia services. A doctor may be responsible for the anesthesia when a partner performs a surgical procedure. Some large practices have their own surgery room, performing the same procedures in the office that they would do in the hospital outpatient surgicenter. In some cases, an anesthesiologist may not be available. Medical billers should become familiar with these codes and the rules for using them. These services may be a significant part of your coding work in the future.

Anesthesia uses some special modifiers to indicate the patient's condition, P1 through P6, and some of the usual CPT modifiers. There are also some 99xxx codes that you bill along with the regular anesthesia service when there are special qualifying circumstances. Keep these special rules in mind as you complete the worksheet.

The descriptions do not specify anesthesia, but all answers should come from this section. Watch for procedures that need a modifier or multiple codes.

1. Cervical diskography injection ____________
2. Abdominal repair, hernia of the diaphragm ____________
3. Delivery of twins, no C-section ____________
4. Radiation therapy requiring general anesthesia ____________
5. Total joint replacement, left ankle, for severe arthritis ____________
6. Open reduction, fracture right humerus ____________
7. Burr holes, critical newborn infant ____________
8. Dual chamber transvenous pacemaker insertion ____________
9. Rhinoplasty, correction of deviated septum ____________
10. Mid-thigh amputation, right leg ____________
11. Harrington rod implant, spinal cord biopsy ____________
12. Rectal endoscopy with biopsy ____________
13. Insert umbrella filter, inferior vena cava ____________
14. Pectus excavatum repair, 4-year-old male ____________
15. Arthroscopy, right shoulder ____________

General Surgery Rules

Surgical procedures on the integumentary system begin the extensive surgery section. CPT provides important guidelines for all surgery. Review them carefully. Then consider the information below as you review the worksheet items.

1. Necessary medical care for diagnostic surgery may be reported separately. Non-diagnostic surgical services include concurrent medical care by the operating surgeon. Other physicians may report medical care that is unrelated to the surgical service. Example: A patient undergoing gallbladder surgery is followed by an internist for chronic emphysema. The internist is paid for the medical care, as it is not related to the surgical service. Medicare has comprehensive tables identifying, by procedure code, the days of medical care included in a surgical service. Other insurers may use the same list or have similar restrictions.
2. Surgical services usually include the local anesthesia administered by the operating surgeon.
3. The payment for the surgery includes all related supplies. The doctor may bill for supplies only if they exceed what is usually required for that service. Insurers may refuse to pay for any additional supplies provided by the surgeon. If the surgery is done in the hospital setting, either inpatient or outpatient, payers assume the hospital provided all the necessary supplies.
4. The subsection information contains the special instructions for using a particular range of codes. In some cases, this vital information may appear on the previous page. Always, after you find the code you seek, review the previous page or two for any special rules related to this coding section.
5. A service that is usually part of another service may, on occasion, be reported as the primary surgery. These codes appear throughout CPT and the description ends with "(separate procedure)." If you perform a service with the (separate procedure) notation, report that service if it is the ONLY service performed or is unrelated to the other procedures or services performed. Use the modifier –59, Distinct Procedural Service, to indicate this service is unrelated to the other procedures or services reported. This is a rule many doctors and billers find confusing.
6. Surgical destruction is usually included in the primary procedure.
7. Use the unlisted procedure code at the end of each surgery section when there is no code for the service performed. New procedures are reported with these codes until a specific code is assigned. If the service involves a new technique for an established procedure, you would usually report the service with the existing code unless the technique is specified in the description. Note that all unlisted procedure codes end in '9' and many end in '99.' Remember, whenever you report these unlisted services, you will need to attach operative notes or provide a complete description of the service.
8. The special report is similar to the unlisted procedure. Again, you must explain the service completely. Documentation must be sent with the claim. These claims may not be sent electronically, as they require attachments.
9. Some of the CPT surgery modifiers are listed in the guidelines of the surgery section. All CPT modifiers appear in Appendix A.
10. Some complications may be reported in addition to the surgery using the modifier –22 and a detailed explanation. Medicare will usually reject any medical care billed by the surgeon during the specified postoperative period. To get paid, the surgeon must establish that the medical care rendered is not part of the usual postoperative care for the previous surgery.

11. Modifiers –54, –55, and –56 cover situations where the surgeon does not provide all the medical care related to the surgery. Physicians other than the surgeon may provide and be paid for medical care related to the surgery if the surgeon indicates his service does not include the preoperative or postoperative medical care.

12. Sometimes the doctor performs multiple procedures. If the surgery is a bilateral carpal tunnel release, you may be instructed by the payer to report the code and the modifier –50, or report two identical lines, one with modifier –RT and the other with modifier –LT. Suppose the patient has gallbladder surgery and the doctor also removes nevi from the neck and left thigh, and a basal cell CA of the scalp. You would report the major procedure on the first line, the basal cell CA on the second line, and the nevi on subsequent lines in the order of diminishing significance. The modifier –51 would be used on all but the first service line. Exception: See 14 below. Also, each service line must show the appropriate diagnosis code reference number.

13. Therapeutic surgery includes all related medical care. The modifier –24 is used when the surgeon performs a separate, postoperative medical service, unrelated to the surgical procedure. Example: A patient had a surgery last week but now visits the surgeon's office for an acute asthma attack. If the asthma is unrelated to the surgery, the office visit may be billed as a separate service with modifier –24.

14. Some multiple surgical procedures must be reported without modifier –51. These are the "add on" codes, identified in CPT Appendix D. Because these codes are added on to the reporting of another code, they can never be used alone. When printing paper claim forms, be sure that these codes do not roll over to be the only service on another claim form.

15. CPT Appendix E lists the CPT codes that are not "add on" codes but do not require the modifier –51. Codes such as 20900 (Bone graft, any donor site, minor or small) or 62284 (Injection procedure for myelography) are billable but assumed to be related to another reported service. In fact, Medicare rejects these codes as incorrectly reported if a –51 modifier is attached.

Modifiers increase in importance each year. Each new edition of CPT and HCPCS bring changes in the familiar ones and new modifiers. Be certain you review the modifier sections when you look for changes in procedure codes.

Medicare and most other payers reject "unbundling," the reporting of multiple services when one code includes all procedures. When physicians code from a list, they may miss a code that contains multiple services. Encounter forms or coding sheets may state:

51840	Marshall-Marchetti
58150	Abdominal Hysterectomy
58700	Salpingectomy(ies)
58940	Oophorectomy(ies)

Turn to code 58150. The description includes codes 58700 and 58940. Suppose the patient with the abdominal hysterectomy also had a Marshall-Marchetti type procedure. The correct code, 58152, contains all the procedures listed above. The CMS rebundling list is called the "Correct Coding Initiative" or CCI and is revised quarterly. Many insurance carriers implement these policies as soon as CMS releases them.

Caution: The CPT worksheets may require multiple procedure codes, a modifier, or the reporting of quantity. Anytime the CPT code says "each," you need to report a quantity, even if it is only one. As you complete the worksheets, pronounce the terms. You can increase your vocabulary as you expand your coding skills.

Integumentary System

These codes include procedures on the skin, subcutaneous and accessory structures, nail, and breast. They cover the removal of lesions, suturing, plastic repairs, burn treatment, and other surgeries. Read the embedded instructions immediately under the headings "Removal of Skin Tags" and "Shaving of Epidermal or Dermal Lesions." Would we report suturing with the shaving of a dermal lesion? No, because the notation states that "the wound does not require suture closure."

Look at CPT's Rule 2 for repairing multiple lacerations. We add together the length of all wounds in the same classification and report the total as a single item. But this rule does not apply to excising multiple lesions, as each is reported individually. A ruler with both inches and centimeters will help you report the correct codes for lesions and suturing.

Before beginning the worksheets, look at the codes and read the text of the entire integumentary section. You may wish to have a medical dictionary and anatomy reference handy. Benign lesions are listed before malignant; suturing is simple, intermediate, and complex; and the miscellaneous categories list services that do not fit into other sections. The integumentary system ends with procedures on the breast.

Note: Watch for worksheet items requiring a modifier, quantity, or multiple codes.

Name ______________________

Integumentary System (10021-19499)

2008 CPT Codes

1. Hair transplant, 21 punch grafts ____________
2. Removal of 8 skin tags from left forearm ____________
3. Implant Norplant contraceptive capsules ____________
4. Simple blepharoplasty, right upper lid ____________
5. Reclosure, three surgical wounds ____________
6. Debridement of skin and subcutaneous tissue, left forearm ____________
7. Permanent removal distal half, left great toenail ____________
8. Full thickness graft 2 x 5 cm., left cheek ____________
9. Simple right shoulder biopsy, single skin lesion ____________
10. Adjacent tissue transfer, trunk, 8 sq. cm. ____________
11. Laser destruction, benign 2 cm. facial lesion ____________
12. Excision/Z-plasty repair, 11 sq. cm. forehead lesion ____________
13. Aspiration, breast cyst, right ____________
14. Burn site preparation of back, 4%, 9 y/o female ____________
15. Wound suture, 3/4" right hand, 1/2" left foot ____________
16. Breast reduction, left ____________
17. Excision, simple repair, right axillary hidradenitis ____________
18. Xenograft, left thigh, 4 x 8 cm. ____________
19. Excise malignant 1/2" lesion, neck ____________
20. I & D hematoma, left hand ____________
21. Major debridement of partial thickness burns, both legs ____________
22. Mohs' technique, 7 tissue blocks, abdomen ____________
23. Fx care, debride left thigh, remove gravel, bone spicules ____________
24. Split autograft, back (2% body area), 2-year-old male ____________
25. Lipectomy, right buttock ____________

Musculoskeletal System

Three worksheets on the musculoskeletal system cover the largest unit in the surgery section. They describe procedures on the supporting structures of the body such as bone, muscle, and tendon. The first worksheet includes trauma, excision/removal, replantation, grafting, the head, neck and thorax, spine, abdomen, and shoulder. The second worksheet has procedures on the arm, hand and fingers, and pelvis and hip joint. The third involves services on the femur, knee, leg, ankle, and foot, and concludes with casting, strapping, and arthroscopy.

The many rules and definitions appearing within the chapter give specific instructions on coding. Note that the service includes the first cast or traction device. This information is repeated at the start of the casting section. There are also modifiers to identify the service as right or left, and ones that identify specific digits.

Some doctors use the terms "closed" and "open" to describe the fracture rather than the treatment. If you believe this is happening in your office, talk to the doctor and get this clarified before billing the service.

The musculoskeletal system is arranged by body site, from the top down, from the center out. After the general procedures, it is organized:

1. Head
2. Neck and thorax
3. Back and flank
4. Spine
5. Abdomen
6. Shoulder
7. Humerus and elbow
8. Forearm and wrist
9. Hand and fingers
10. Pelvis and hip joint
11. Femur and knee joint
12. Leg and ankle joint
13. Foot

Each body site section follows this organization:

1. Incision
2. Excision
3. Introduction or removal
4. Repair, revision, reconstruction
5. Fracture and/or dislocation
6. Manipulation
7. Arthrodesis
8. Amputation
9. Miscellaneous

Note how many worksheet items in the musculoskeletal section contain the diagnosis. Watch for items that need multiple procedure codes, right, left, finger, and toe modifiers, or quantity specified.

Name ____________________________

Musculoskeletal System – I (20000-23929)

2008 CPT Codes

1. Percutaneous needle biopsy, right deltoid muscle ____________
2. Partial acromionectomy, left ____________
3. Wick monitoring, muscle compartment syndrome, right leg ____________
4. Four segment kyphectomy ____________
5. Injection service for left TMJ arthrogram ____________
6. LeFort II reconstruction, 2 autografts ____________
7. Removal of right shoulder prosthesis for replacement ____________
8. Fracture of mandible, dental fixation, closed ____________
9. Maxillectomy, intra-extra oral osteotomy, for cyst ____________
10. Radical sternal resection with major bone graft for osteomyelitis (two codes) ____________
11. Remove external wire fixation under anesthesia ____________
12. Open fractures, two thoracic vertebrae ____________
13. Right shoulder arthrodesis, no graft ____________
14. Care of simple nasal fracture ____________
15. Right total shoulder ____________
16. Reattachment of total amputation of right thumb tip ____________
17. Anterior osteotomy, diskectomy, 2 thoracic vertebrae (two codes) ____________
18. Medrol injection, right hip ____________
19. Exploratory arthrotomy, left A-C joint ____________
20. Open treatment blowout fracture, right orbit ____________
21. Microvascular anastomosis, osteocutaneous flap, left great toe ____________
22. Custom prosthesis preparation, left ear ____________
23. Explore right chest, multiple gunshot wounds ____________
24. Incision deep soft tissue, osteomyelitic abscess, left buttock ____________
25. Exploration of fusion, lumbar spine ____________

Name ____________________

Musculoskeletal System – II (23930-27299)

2008 CPT Codes

1. Open repair of left Dupuytren's contracture ____________
2. Hypothenar opponensplasty, right ____________
3. Open Bennett fracture with external fixation, left ____________
4. Secondary flexor repair and graft, right no man's land ____________
5. Synovial biopsy of right elbow by arthrotomy ____________
6. Manipulation lunate dislocation, closed ____________
7. Darrach procedure, left ____________
8. Decompression fasciotomy, extensor, left wrist ____________
9. Fx left olecranon, external fixation, open treatment ____________
10. Right Z-plasty fasciectomy with release of 3rd and 4th IP joints (multiple codes) ____________
11. Repair nonunion of left radius without graft ____________
12. Treatment of traumatic left hip dislocation, no anesthesia ____________
13. Flap repair, syndactyly, right 4th web space ____________
14. Removal of recurrent ganglion, left wrist ____________
15. Transmetacarpal reamputation, left first finger ____________
16. Subfascial soft tissue biopsy, right forearm ____________
17. Manipulation with pin, left epicondylar fracture ____________
18. Closed manipulation MP dislocation left 4th finger, with anesthesia ____________
19. Saucerization distal phalanx, left ring finger ____________
20. Total hip replacement, right ____________
21. Remove implant, revise arthroplasty, left wrist ____________
22. Opposition fusion and graft, left thumb ____________
23. Microvascular toe-to-hand transfer 2nd and 3rd toe to previous bone graft, left hand ____________
24. Right femur, epiphyseal arrest by stapling ____________
25. Reinsert ruptured left distal triceps tendon with graft ____________

Name ______________________

Musculoskeletal System – III (27301-29999)

2008 CPT Codes

1. Right shoulder arthroscopy with lysis of adhesions ____________
2. Phalangectomy, left third toe ____________
3. Exploration with synovial biopsy by arthrotomy, left knee ____________
4. Release of left tarsal tunnel ____________
5. Left knee arthroscopy, sewing needle removed ____________
6. Fracture right medial malleolus, closed, no manipulation ____________
7. Surgical correction with fixation, left patellar fracture ____________
8. Gastrocnemius neurectomy, left ____________
9. Heyman midtarsal capsulotomy, right ____________
10. Lengthening bilateral hamstring tendons ____________
11. I & D hematoma, left ankle ____________
12. Repair of Risser jacket ____________
13. Fracture femoral shaft, open with screws, left ____________
14. Right Joplin bunion repair ____________
15. Repair of severed collateral ligament, right ankle ____________
16. Knock-knee osteotomy, left, before closure ____________
17. Lengthening, left Achilles tendon ____________
18. Plantar fasciotomy, left, by arthroscopy ____________
19. Goldwaite procedure for dislocating patella, right ____________
20. Manipulation right trimalleolar fracture ____________
21. Guillotine amputation, left tibia/fibula ____________
22. Application of right long arm splint ____________
23. Left sesamoid fracture, closed treatment ____________
24. Revision right long leg cast, walker heel applied ____________
25. Right great toe IP joint arthrodesis ____________

Respiratory System

From nosebleed and tonsillectomy to removal of a lung, this section covers procedures associated with the nose, sinuses, larynx, trachea, bronchi, lungs, and pleura.

In this system we are introduced to endoscopy. Note that when a surgical or therapeutic endoscopy is performed, the appropriate sinusotomy, diagnostic endoscopy, and inspecting all sinuses is included. This is another example of correct coding, or bundling of services.

Name ______________________

Respiratory System (30000-32999)

2008 CPT Codes

1. Partial removal, left inferior turbinate ______
2. Split cricoid laryngoplasty ______
3. Endoscopy with A&P ethmoidectomy ______
4. Closure nasoseptal perforations from cocaine ______
5. Bronchoscopy with laser destruction of lesions ______
6. Tube thoracostomy for empyema ______
7. External arytenoidopexy ______
8. Revision of tracheostoma ______
9. Parietal pleurectomy ______
10. Intranasal antrotomy ______
11. Plastic repair closure of tracheostomy ______
12. Intrathoracic tracheoplasty ______
13. Tracheostomy tracheobronchoscopy ______
14. Direct laryngoscopy with biopsy, via microscope ______
15. Surgical nasal endoscopy, polypectomy ______
16. Secondary major rhinoplasty ______
17. Removal of toy from nose, 2 y/o male, in office ______
18. Pneumonolysis with packing ______
19. Radical neck, partial laryngectomy for CA ______
20. Sinusotomy, four sinuses ______
21. Polypectomy, office surgery ______
22. Empyemectomy ______
23. Surgical endoscopy, repair sphenoid CSF leak ______
24. Thoracoscopy, bilateral wedge resection ______
25. Puncture aspiration, left lung ______

Cardiovascular System

This section lists the surgical procedures on the vascular and cardiac systems: the heart, veins, and arteries. The instructional introductory paragraphs refer to first, second, and third order vessels and vascular families, and the injection procedures for arteriography.

The Society of Interventional Radiology (SIR) distributes an excellent reference explaining the family trees of the vascular system. This manual is available on their website:

http://directory.sirweb.org/store/

Because surgery on the cardiovascular system usually represents major surgery, there are few codes identified as "separate procedure." Operations on the arteries and veins include the arteriogram. Aortic procedures include the sympathectomy, if performed. Diagnostic cardiac catheterization is in the Medicine section.

Review the extensive explanation of pacemaker and cardioverter-defibrillator services. Coronary bypass grafting, both venous and arterial, is complex and requires careful reading.

Caution: Watch out for worksheet item 3. Move slowly and carefully through this CPT section.

Name ______________________

Cardiovascular System (33010-37799)

2008 CPT Codes

1. Long and short saphenous vein stripping, left leg ____________
2. Vein graft repair, left brachial artery ____________
3. Coronary bypass grafts, 1 venous and 2 arterial ____________
4. Direct repair of vertebral artery aneurysm ____________
5. Revision of pacemaker pocket ____________
6. Removal of fragment, broken arterial catheter ____________
7. Open atrial septostomy with bypass ____________
8. Insertion AV sequential pacemaker ____________
9. Needle placement, left jugular vein ____________
10. Removal of implanted arterial infusion pump ____________
11. Pulmonary embolectomy without bypass ____________
12. Mitral valvotomy with bypass ____________
13. Cardiectomy with heart transplant ____________
14. Intracatheter AV shunt for dialysis ____________
15. Diagnostic arterial puncture ____________
16. Cutdown venipuncture, infant ____________
17. Splenorenal bypass, synthetic graft ____________
18. Percutaneous transluminal fem-pop atherectomy ____________
19. Direct repair of ruptured splenic artery aneurysm ____________
20. Intrauterine fetal transfusion ____________
21. Repeat pericardiocentesis ____________
22. Repair lacerated aorta with bypass ____________
23. Resection with commissurotomy for infundibular stenosis ____________
24. Ligation/repair patent ductus arteriosus, 19 y/o female ____________
25. Patch closure of ventricular septal defect ____________

Hemic and Lymphatic - Mediastinum and Diaphragm

These combined, small sections include procedures on the spleen, bone marrow, stem cell services/procedures, lymph nodes and channels, mediastinum, and diaphragm.

Compared to the cardiovascular section, this one is easy.

Name ________________________

Hemic and Lymphatic - Mediastinum and Diaphragm (38100-39599)

2008 CPT Codes

1. Superficial needle biopsy of inguinal lymph node ____________
2. Complete right axillary lymphadenectomy ____________
3. Repair acute traumatic hernia of diaphragm ____________
4. Insertion of thoracic duct cannula ____________
5. Drainage of single lymph node abscess, left axilla ____________
6. Thoracoabdominal repair, hiatal hernia ____________
7. Excision of deep axillary node, right ____________
8. Radical retroperitoneal lymphadenectomy ____________
9. Lymphangiotomy ____________
10. Mediastinoscopy with biopsy ____________
11. Partial splenectomy for traumatic injury ____________
12. Superficial inguino-femoral lymphadenectomy ____________
13. Retroperitoneal staging lymphadenectomy ____________
14. Correct newborn diaphragmatic hernia, insert chest tube ____________
15. Needle bone marrow biopsy ____________
16. Suprahyoid lymphadenectomy ____________
17. Eventration of paralytic diaphragm ____________
18. Deep jugular node dissection x 3 ____________
19. Allogenic bone marrow transplant ____________
20. Injection for lymphangiography ____________
21. Removal of benign neoplasm from mediastinum ____________
22. Staging, partial pelvic lymphadenectomy ____________
23. Excise left axillary hygroma, deep neurovascular dissection ____________
24. Repair ruptured spleen ____________
25. Total pelvic lymphadenectomy by laparoscope ____________

Digestive System

This system covers procedures on the mouth, salivary glands, pharynx, adenoids, tonsils, esophagus, stomach, intestines, appendix, rectum and anus, liver, biliary tract, pancreas, abdomen, peritoneum, omentum, and hernia repair.

This diverse section contains endoscopic procedures and refers to the related radiographic guidance, supervision and interpretation services. Remember that surgical endoscopy includes diagnostic endoscopy.

Watch for multiple codes and the item that requires a modifier.

Name ______________________

Digestive System (40490-49999)

2008 CPT Codes

1. I & D peritonsillar abscess ________
2. Flexible esophagoscopy with removal of FB ________
3. Roux-en-Y bypass for obesity ________
4. Fredet-Ramstedt pyloromyotomy ________
5. Transanal hemicolectomy ________
6. Commando glossectomy ________
7. Initial inguinal hernia repair, 4-year-old male ________
8. Transsacral proctectomy ________
9. Simple ligature hemorrhoidectomy ________
10. ERCP with pancreatic duct stent ________
11. Stomal colonoscopy for hemorrhage ________
12. Upper GI endoscopy, dilate obstructed outlet ________
13. Staging laparotomy for Hodgkins, with intraoperative tube jejunostomy ________
14. Second stage, primary bilateral cleft lip repair ________
15. Total arch vestibuloplasty ________
16. Subsequent peritoneal lavage ________
17. Rectal stricture dilation under general anesthesia ________
18. Cholecystectomy with cholangiography ________
19. Thoracic closure of esophagostomy ________
20. Flexible sigmoidoscopy for biopsy ________
21. Partial left lobe hepatectomy ________
22. Salivary gland biopsy by incision ________
23. Hepaticoenterostomy, by U-tube ________
24. Removal of dental implant, left mandible ________
25. Plastic repair of pharynx ________

Urinary System

This section includes the procedures on the kidney, ureter, bladder, and urethra; also transplant services, including the harvesting of the kidney. Urinary endoscopy and other procedures identify special bundling instructions.

Caution: Read the worksheet items carefully. Urethra and ureter can look similar in some forms of the words. Note the different codes for male and female.

One worksheet item has two possible codes. What else do you need to know to find the exact code?

Name ____________________

Urinary System (50010-53899)

2008 CPT Codes

1. Subsequent urethral stricture dilation, male, age 27 ____________
2. Transurethral resection of prostate ____________
3. Closure of traumatic kidney wound ____________
4. Infant meatotomy ____________
5. Cystourethroscopy, fulguration of 1.9 cm. tumor ____________
6. Complete cystectomy, bilateral lymphadenectomy ____________
7. Bowel anastomosis with ureterocolon conduit ____________
8. Repair of ureterovisceral fistula ____________
9. EMG anal sphincter ____________
10. Subsequent dilation urethra, female, age 21 ____________
11. Cystourethroscopy, steroid treatment of stricture ____________
12. Suprapubic catheter aspiration of bladder ____________
13. Exploratory nephrotomy ____________
14. Partial excision of left kidney ____________
15. Excision of Cowper's gland ____________
16. Sling procedure for incontinence, male, age 43 ____________
17. Ureterolithotomy, stone in upper third ____________
18. Plastic repair of ureter for stricture ____________
19. Litholapaxy, 2.7 cm. calculus ____________
20. Marshall-Marchetti-Kranz procedure ____________
21. Cystometrogram ____________
22. Injection procedure for chain urethrocystography ____________
23. Percutaneous placement of ureteral stent ____________
24. Bilateral pyeloplasty for horseshoe kidney, left ____________
25. Laser vaporization of prostate with TURP ____________

Male Genital System

These codes identify procedures on the penis, testis, epididymis, tunica vaginalis, scrotum, vas deferens, spermatic cord, seminal vesicles, and prostate.

Watch for the worksheet item that has two possible answers.

Name ____________________

Male Genital System (54000-55899)

2008 CPT Codes

1. Newborn clamp circumcision ________
2. Traumatic partial amputation of penis ________
3. Punch biopsy of prostate ________
4. Bilateral hydrocelectomy ________
5. Radical retropubic prostatectomy ________
6. Urethroplasty, third stage Cecil repair ________
7. Electroejaculation ________
8. Implantation of prosthetic testicle ________
9. Bilateral vasectomy ________
10. Chemical destruction of penile condyloma ________
11. Exploration of scrotum ________
12. Complex scrotoplasty ________
13. Insertion of radioactive pellet in prostate ________
14. One stage repair, perineal hypospadias with tube ________
15. Radical orchiectomy, abdominal exploration ________
16. Insertion of inflatable penile prosthesis ________
17. Abdominal vesiculectomy ________
18. Varicocelectomy with hernia repair ________
19. Abdominal exploration for undescended testis ________
20. Plethysmography of penis ________
21. Biopsy and exploration of epididymis ________
22. Testicular biopsy via needle ________
23. Bilateral venous shunt for priapism ________
24. Complex prostatotomy for abscess ________
25. Vasovasorrhaphy ________

Intersex, Female Genital, and Maternity

This section defines reproductive system procedures, intersex surgery, procedures on the vulva, perineum and introitus, vagina, cervix and corpus uteri, oviduct, ovary, and in vitro fertilization. Also included are the services related to delivery, antepartum, and postpartum care.

There are several options for endoscopy in this section. You may need to read the procedure notes to code the vulvar surgery as simple, radical, partial, or complete.

Note the services included in the prenatal or antepartum care. The instructions state: "other visits or services within this time period should be coded separately." This means that if you see a maternity patient for the flu or a burn, and you code it as unrelated to the pregnancy, you may bill it as an additional service. Would you bill inpatient medical care for the time your patient is hospitalized for delivery? No, not for the usual care associated with delivery, but you could report additional care for other complications. Also, another physician, following the patient for an unrelated difficulty, such as a cardiac problem, would bill for regular medical care as it is not related to the delivery.

Examine the instructions on partial prenatal care. Note that "abortion," not miscarriage, is the correct term for an incompleted pregnancy. Abortions may be spontaneous, missed, septic, or induced.

Some worksheet items may require multiple codes or quantity indicators.

Name ____________________________

Intersex, Female Genital, and Maternity (55920-59899)

2008 CPT Codes

1. Removal of 3 small leiomyomata by laparoscopy ____________
2. Repair of rectovaginal fistula with colostomy ____________
3. Intrauterine embryo transfer ____________
4. Sex change surgery, female to male ____________
5. Cervical LEEP biopsy, small electrode ____________
6. Tubal occlusion with ring ____________
7. Treatment of second trimester missed abortion ____________
8. Cystocele/urethrocele repair ____________
9. Chorionic villus sampling by needle ____________
10. Laparoscopic excision of pelvic lesions ____________
11. Injection of dye for hysterosalpingogram ____________
12. Salpingectomy for ectopic pregnancy, by laparoscopy ____________
13. Vaginal delivery with tocolysis ____________
14. Vaginal excision, 3 uterine fibroids, 240 grams ____________
15. Cervical stump excision, repair of pelvic floor ____________
16. Vaginal hysterectomy, partial colpectomy, enterocele repair ____________
17. Vaginal trachelorrhaphy ____________
18. Laser destruction of extensive vaginal lesions ____________
19. Complete pelvic exenteration ____________
20. Bilateral excision of ovarian cysts ____________
21. C-section delivery with postpartum care ____________
22. Tubal ligation, 1 day after delivery ____________
23. Fascial sling for stress incontinence ____________
24. Biopsy perineum, two lesions ____________
25. Hysteroscopy, lysis of adhesions ____________

Endocrine and Nervous Systems

Procedures on the thyroid, parathyroid, thymus and adrenal glands, carotid body, skull, meninges and brain, spine and spinal cord, extracranial and peripheral nerves, and autonomic nervous system; destruction by neurolytic agent, neuroplasty, and neurorrhaphy are included on this worksheet.

The Nervous System surgery is categorized by approach, definitive surgery, and reconstruction services, and may be performed by more than one surgeon. You may want to refer to an anatomy text for clarification of the complex neurosurgical procedures.

Caution: Worksheet items 6 and 23. Don't forget modifiers and quantity where needed.

Name ____________________________

Endocrine and Nervous Systems (60000-64999)

2008 CPT Codes

1. Subtotal thyroidectomy with radical neck dissection ____________
2. Transcranial orbital exploration, removal of bullet ____________
3. Intra-abdominal avulsion, vagus nerve ____________
4. Laminectomy and excision of intradural sacral lesion ____________
5. Single nerve graft, left arm, 4.5 cm. ____________
6. Injection procedure, lumbar diskogram (L4-L5) ____________
7. Decompressive resection, single cervical vertebral body ____________
8. Remove and replace CSF shunt system ____________
9. Percutaneous stereotactic chemical lesion, trigeminal ____________
10. Excision of thyroid adenoma ____________
11. Paracervical nerve block for delivery ____________
12. Repeat subdural tap through suture ____________
13. Excise and graft of infected intradural bone ____________
14. Total removal of implanted spinal neurostimulator ____________
15. Bone flap craniotomy for cerebellopontine tumor ____________
16. Suture thenar motor nerve, right hand ____________
17. Exploratory burr hole, supratentorial ____________
18. Repair complex dural intracranial AV malformation ____________
19. Cervical hemilaminectomy/re-exploration & decompression ____________
20. Brain stem biopsy, transoral/split mandible approach ____________
21. Excision of carotid body tumor and artery ____________
22. Craniectomy for posterior fossa tumor ____________
23. Cable nerve grafts, 3 cm. left arm, 4.5 cm. left leg ____________
24. LeFort osteotomy with fixation, anterior fossa ____________
25. Cranioplasty for 6.5 cm. skull lesion ____________

Eye and Ocular Adnexa

This section lists procedures on the eyeball, cornea, iris, ciliary body, lens, vitreous, retina, eye muscles, bony orbit, eyelids, conjunctiva, and lacrimal system.

Note the distinction between ocular and orbital implants. There are many laser procedures for the eye. Removal of a cataract may include other services. The surgeon may do the lens implant as a single stage procedure, at the time the cataract is removed, or later.

To code accurately, what more do you need to know about item 9? Watch for add-on or multiple codes and modifiers.

Name ____________________

Eye and Ocular Adnexa (65091-68899)

2008 CPT Codes

1. Probe/irrigate left nasolacrimal duct under general ____________
2. One laser treatment session, 3 small retinal breaks, left ____________
3. Exploration left orbit, remove embedded nailhead ____________
4. Excise 0.75 cm. conjunctival lesion, left eye ____________
5. Reinsert ocular implant with conjunctival graft, right ____________
6. Revise operative site, right anterior segment ____________
7. Removal of posterior FB with magnet, left eye ____________
8. Left tarsal wedge excision for ectropion ____________
9. Iridectomy for glaucoma, left ____________
10. Correction of right surgical astigmatism by wedge ____________
11. External levator repair, right blepharoptosis ____________
12. Enucleation, insertion of muscle stabilized implant, left ____________
13. Repeat scleral buckling, old retinal detachment, left ____________
14. Excise lower lid chalazions, 3 left, 1 right ____________
15. Right corneal laceration repair with tissue glue ____________
16. Laser treatment of left vitreous strands ____________
17. Removal of right dacryolith ____________
18. Laser trabeculoplasty, right ____________
19. Discission of left secondary cataract by incision ____________
20. Total reconstruction, right upper lid ____________
21. Extracapsular phacoemulsification with lens implant, left ____________
22. Posterior fixation for strabismus, resect 2 horizontal muscles, right eye ____________
23. Plug closure, right lacrimal punctum ____________
24. Bilateral antibiotic injection, anterior chamber ____________
25. Initial superior oblique strabismus surgery, left ____________

Auditory System

This section includes procedures on the external, middle, and inner ear, and the temporal bone. After the eye, coding the ear services seems easy.

Caution: One worksheet item needs an add-on code, most need modifiers.

Name ____________________________

Auditory System (69000-69990)

2008 CPT Codes

1. Replace left temporal bone conduction device ____________
2. Bilateral otoplasty for severely protruding ears ____________
3. Total facial nerve repair and graft, by operating microscope ____________
4. Repeat right mastoidectomy, now radical ____________
5. Excision of right external ear cyst ____________
6. Neurectomy, right tympanic membrane ____________
7. Postauricular middle ear exploration, left ____________
8. Subtotal mastoidectomy, right ____________
9. Semicircular canal fenestration, left ____________
10. Stapedotomy, repair of right ossicular chain ____________
11. Catheterize/inflate eustachian tube, transnasal ____________
12. Right oval window fistula repair ____________
13. Facial nerve repair, medial/geniculate, left ____________
14. Left tube tympanostomy with Novocaine ____________
15. Subtotal amputation, right external ear ____________
16. Cochlear implant, right ____________
17. Excision polyp, left ear ____________
18. Remove FB left external ear, general anesthesia ____________
19. I&D of abscess, left external meatus ____________
20. Myringoplasty, right ____________
21. Left mastoidectomy with labyrinthectomy ____________
22. Excision of neoplasm, left temporal bone ____________
23. Mastoidectomy/tympanoplasty, reconstruct Rt ossicular chain ____________
24. Excision left extratemporal glomus tumor ____________
25. Routine cleaning of right mastoid cavity ____________

Radiology

The first worksheet of radiographic procedures covers the section on diagnostic radiology and imaging. It includes flat films of the head and neck, chest, spine, pelvis, and upper and lower extremities. These studies are the most common radiologic procedures performed in the physician's office.

Worksheet II includes studies of the abdomen, gastrointestinal and urinary tracts, and gynecological and obstetrical services. It also includes diagnostic imaging of the heart, aorta and arteries, and veins and lymphatics. It concludes with transcatheter procedures, transluminal atherectomy, and other therapeutic procedures.

The third worksheet covers three sections. The first section, diagnostic ultrasound or "echo," includes procedures for diagnosis and guidance. The second section, radiation oncology, provides codes for clinical treatment planning, delivery and management, hyperthermia, and brachytherapy. The last section, diagnostic nuclear medicine, has codes for the endocrine, lymphatic, gastrointestinal, musculoskeletal, cardiovascular, respiratory, nervous, and genitourinary systems, and therapeutic nuclear studies.

Radiology services, the 70000 codes, are one of the non-surgical sections in CPT. The section has special instructions, unlisted procedure codes, and modifiers. The "supervision and interpretation" services correspond to many of the injection procedures in previous surgical sections. Many of the "S&I" codes are followed by a reference to the surgical part of the diagnostic service. The Interventional Radiology Coding Users' Guide is very helpful in explaining these services.

Many specialists perform S&I studies, not just radiologists. Note that a written report, signed by the doctor interpreting the study, is part of the service and may not be billed separately. Nuclear medicine, once limited to the hospital setting, is now part of some medical practices.

Remember that the service at the doctor's office is the global or complete service. The same study performed at the hospital must be reported as the "professional component." With very few exceptions, when the place of service is 21 (inpatient), 22 (outpatient), or 23 (emergency department), the 7xxxx service will require the modifier –26.

Move slowly through this section, reading all instructions and definitions. If you are confused by words ending in "gram" or "graphy," think of telegram and telegraphy. One is the result, the other the process.

Watch for items requiring modifiers or multiple codes.

Name ____________________________

Radiology – I (70010-73725)

2008 CPT Codes

1. S&I arthrography, left knee ____________
2. 4 views, nasal fracture ____________
3. X-ray of right knee, 4 views ____________
4. CT of pelvis, with contrast ____________
5. Neck CT with contrast and additional sections ____________
6. Pelvis, 2 views ____________
7. X-ray left eye, no foreign body ____________
8. Scoliosis x-ray study of the spine ____________
9. Chest x-ray, 1 view ____________
10. TMJ arthrography, with supervision/interpretation ____________
11. S&I pacemaker insertion ____________
12. 2 views right 4th and 5th fingers ____________
13. Cervical MRI, no contrast ____________
14. X-ray teeth, right upper, left upper and lower ____________
15. 2 views cervical spine, outpatient ____________
16. Right leg x-ray, 2-month-old baby boy ____________
17. Bilateral fractured ribs, 3 views ____________
18. X-ray elbow, PA and Lateral ____________
19. Complete study left hip ____________
20. Head MRI, no contrast, inpatient ____________
21. X-ray exam left scapula, 3 views ____________
22. CT thoracic spine with contrast ____________
23. Proton imaging for lymph nodes, chest ____________
24. X-ray right sialolith ____________
25. Cervical myelogram, S&I ____________

Name ______________________

Radiology – II (74000-76499)

2008 CPT Codes

1. CT guidance for stereotactic localization ____________
2. Bilateral selective adrenal venography, S&I ____________
3. Videography of swallowing ____________
4. Acute abdomen series ____________
5. Cineradiography in operating room ____________
6. Bilateral selective adrenal angiography, S&I ____________
7. Supervise/interpret voiding urethrocystography ____________
8. Bilateral femoral intravascular ultrasound ____________
9. S&I, transcatheter removal of broken catheter ____________
10. LeVeen shuntogram S&I ____________
11. Barium enema, KUB study ____________
12. Contrast monitoring to change percutaneous drain tube, S&I ____________
13. S&I bilateral carotid neck angiogram ____________
14. Retrograde urography with KUB ____________
15. Percutaneous transhepatic portography, S&I, in ER ____________
16. S&I, transluminal renal atherectomy ____________
17. Supervise/interpret AV shunt angiogram ____________
18. S&I bilateral selective renal angiography ____________
19. Thoracic aortography by serialography, S&I ____________
20. Perineogram ____________
21. Lymphangiography, right arm, S&I ____________
22. Consult/report on x-rays done at University Hospital ____________
23. Orthoroentgenogram ____________
24. Bilateral screening mammogram ____________
25. Cardiac MRI and stress imaging, with contrast ____________

Name ________________________

Radiology – III (76506-79999)

2008 CPT Codes

1. Complete obstetrical B-scan, twin pregnancy ____________
2. Thyroid, metastatic CA imaging, total ____________
3. Simulation treatment planning, right hip and knee ____________
4. SPECT cardiac rest and exercise studies at hospital ____________
5. Lymph gland imaging ____________
6. Voiding cystogram reflux study with residual bladder study ____________
7. Radiation treatment: L shoulder & hip, 7.5 MeV ____________
8. Pulmonary ventilation and perfusion study, quantitative ____________
9. Transrectal echo ____________
10. Intracavitary element placement, 11 ribbons, outpatient ____________
11. Combined B-12 absorption study ____________
12. Radioelement placement, surface of left forearm ____________
13. Ophthalmic biometry A-scan ____________
14. External hyperthermia, 2.7 cm. deep ____________
15. Splenic red cell survival measurement ____________
16. First pass cardiac resting study ____________
17. Brachytherapy planning, two sources ____________
18. SPECT bone imaging, professional component only ____________
19. Radiopharmaceutical treatment via joint infusion ____________
20. Ultrasound guidance for needle biopsy, S&I ____________
21. Radionuclide localization, lung abscess ____________
22. PET tumor imaging, professional component ____________
23. Repeat fetal Doppler echocardiogram ____________
24. Ultrasound guidance for amniocentesis, S&I ____________
25. SPECT liver imaging ____________

Pathology and Laboratory

Lab worksheet Part I covers lab panels, drug testing, therapeutic drug assays, evocative/suppression testing, clinical pathology consultations, urinalysis, and ends with chemistry tests. Note that the chemistry tests are listed in alphabetic order.

Part II includes molecular diagnostics, hematology, coagulation, immunology, and tissue typing.

The final lab worksheet describes transfusion medicine, microbiology, anatomic pathology, including postmortem examination and cytopathology, cytogenics, surgical pathology, and miscellaneous laboratory services, ending with reproductive medicine procedures.

Reimbursement varies widely for laboratory studies. Review the manuals for the office testing equipment to determine the correct code for each study. Do not take the word of the equipment salesperson.

A federal regulation, the Clinical Laboratory Improvement Act (CLIA), rated laboratory tests by complexity. Each lab is certified to perform a specified level of testing. Some physicians discontinued all office laboratory work. Other practices reduced their laboratory work to only basic, uncomplicated services.

As you complete the worksheets, review the guidelines and look for instructions within each subsection. A few codes include the physician's services. Watch for the lab tests with legal implications. Unlike the surgical services, the clinical laboratory tests may be numbered so that the lowest code number identifies the most comprehensive study. A few even describe testing you can do safely at home.

Some worksheet items require multiple codes or quantity reporting.

Name ____________________

Pathology and Laboratory – I (80047-83887)

2008 CPT Codes

1. Four studies each, lutenizing hormone and FSH ________
2. Quantitative theophylline screen, blood ________
3. Occult blood in stool, three guaiac test cards ________
4. Qualitative cystine/homocystine, urine ________
5. Urinary amino acids, quantitative, 3 specimens ________
6. Glucose tolerance test, 4 specimens ________
7. Blood ethanol levels ________
8. Semen analysis for fructose ________
9. Atomic spectroscopy, manganese ________
10. HDL cholesterol direct measurement ________
11. Manual microscopic urinalysis ________
12. Blood catecholamines ________
13. Creatinine clearance ________
14. Obstetric panel of tests ________
15. Hemoglobin, methemoglobin, qualitative ________
16. Folic acid RBC ________
17. Cocaine drug screening ________
18. Estriol ________
19. Color pregnancy test, urine ________
20. Total serum cholesterol ________
21. Hepatitis ABC antibodies, B surface antigens ________
22. Fractionation (17-KS) ketosteroids ________
23. CRH stimulation panel ________
24. Mucopolysaccharide screen ________
25. TSH panel, 4 studies, two hours ________

Name ____________________

Pathology and Laboratory – II (83890-86849)

2008 CPT Codes

1. Total blood protein, Western Blot ____________
2. Quantitative D-dimer degraded fibrin ____________
3. PKU blood test, 2-day-old infant ____________
4. Routine prothrombin time ____________
5. Vitamin E ____________
6. Total T cell with absolute CD4 and 8 ____________
7. Single nucleic acid probe ____________
8. Eastern equine encephalitis antibody test ____________
9. Clotting factor VIII, single stage ____________
10. Vitamin B-2 ____________
11. C-reactive protein ____________
12. Parathyroid hormone ____________
13. Heparin neutralization ____________
14. HLA typing, A, single antigen ____________
15. Strip test, urea nitrogen ____________
16. Skin test for histoplasmosis ____________
17. Chorionic gonadotropin, qualitative ____________
18. Hepatitis C antibody ____________
19. Total testosterone ____________
20. Platelet antibody identification ____________
21. Urinary potassium ____________
22. Total clotting inhibitor, protein S ____________
23. Blood/urine Xylose absorption test ____________
24. Rubella antibody screen ____________
25. Double strand DNA antibody ____________

Name ______________________

Pathology and Laboratory – III (86850-89356)

2008 CPT Codes

1. Platelet pooling ____________
2. Bone marrow tissue analysis for malignancy ____________
3. Scanning electron microscopy ____________
4. Stool culture for *salmonella* ____________
5. Coroner ordered autopsy ____________
6. Surgical pathology, gross/micro, uterus with tumor ____________
7. Flow cytometry, DNA analysis ____________
8. Rabbit inoculation, observation ____________
9. Influenza detection by immunoassay ____________
10. Gross autopsy, including brain ____________
11. Surgical pathology, gross/micro cholesteatoma ____________
12. Preoperative autologous blood collection/storage ____________
13. Complete semen analysis ____________
14. Consult/report on slides from University Hospital ____________
15. Antibiotic sensitivity study, 10 disks ____________
16. Chlamydia culture ____________
17. Limited chromosome analysis/banding, amniotic fluid ____________
18. KOH skin slide prep ____________
19. Forensic cytopathology for sperm ____________
20. CSF cell count with differential ____________
21. Thawing fresh frozen plasma, 2 units ____________
22. Three hour gastric secretory study ____________
23. Preparations for nerve teasing ____________
24. Collection of vaginal smear for dark field exam ____________
25. Intraoperative consultation and frozen section, two specimens ____________

Medicine

Worksheet I covers injections, psychiatry, dialysis services, diagnostic medical services for gastroenterology, and non-surgical procedures on the eye and ear.

The second worksheet has cardiovascular and pulmonary diagnostic and therapeutic services, procedures for allergy, and neurology.

Worksheet III includes chemotherapy and physical medicine. The special services of osteopaths and chiropractors, additional anesthesia codes, and other special procedures and services are the final subsections of CPT. The recently added Category II and III codes may not be accepted by all insurance plans. Some of the special services, procedures, and reports also may be excluded from payment.

Many CPTs ago, office visits were part of the Medicine section. Then they became evaluation and management services and are now listed separately. The invasive procedures in this section are diagnostic and are usually considered non-surgical. This may seem strange since coronary angioplasty, the procedure some people have instead of open-heart surgery, is in this section.

Many doctors use services from this section such as injections, EKGs, and pulmonary function testing. Generally, as you can see from the subsection listing, these services belong to a medical specialty. Study these services carefully. The guidelines for this section are familiar. Now we apply them to medical procedures rather than surgery.

Caution: Watch for multiple codes, modifiers, and quantity reporting.

Name ________________________

Medicine – I (90281-92700)

2008 CPT Codes

1. Endothelial microscopy, cell count, photo/report ____________
2. Medical hypnotherapy to stop smoking ____________
3. Intravenous push injection ____________
4. Glaucoma water provocation test with tonogram ____________
5. Rhinomanometry ____________
6. Binaural hearing aid exam ____________
7. Manometric studies, anus and rectum ____________
8. Bernstein test for esophagitis ____________
9. Tangent screen visual fields, right eye ____________
10. Tetanus vaccine, 27-year-old male, jet injector ____________
11. Hepatitis B immunization series, 18 y/o dialysis patient ____________
12. Biofeedback training for arrhythmia ____________
13. Monthly dialysis monitoring, 16 y/o female ____________
14. Psychotherapy, 1 hour, 15 minutes ____________
15. Psychotherapy with family, patient absent ____________
16. Comprehensive eye exam, new patient ____________
17. Fluorescein angiography, complete ____________
18. Contact lens replacement, right ____________
19. Tympanometry ____________
20. Dialysis training, one session ____________
21. Air audiometry ____________
22. Fitting of bifocal lenses ____________
23. Multiple seizure electroconvulsive treatments, one session ____________
24. Audiometry by select picture ____________
25. Inpatient nonverbal psychotherapy with medical visit, 45 minutes ____________

Name ______________________

Medicine – II (92950-96020)

2008 CPT Codes

1. Coronary thrombolysis by IV infusion ____________
2. Inpatient right and left heart cath, congenital heart defect ____________
3. Interp/report only, tilt table cardiac testing ____________
4. Pulmonary percutaneous balloon valvuloplasty ____________
5. EMG/NCT, cranial nerve supplied muscles, bilateral ____________
6. Dispense 15 doses antigen, bee & wasp ____________
7. Brief study, transcranial Doppler ____________
8. Cardiac stress test, tracing only ____________
9. Awake/sleep EEG, 10 p.m. to 7 a.m. ____________
10. CPAP ____________
11. Scratch tests, 10 trees, 3 venom ____________
12. Skin electromyography, 10 muscles, running on treadmill ____________
13. 24 hour ECG, miniature, recording only ____________
14. Complete service, 1 month patient activated spirometry recording ____________
15. Repeat analysis of cranial nerve stimulator implant ____________
16. Myasthenia gravis tensilon test ____________
17. His Bundle recording ____________
18. Interpret/report total body plethysmography ____________
19. Venous Doppler, both legs, complete study ____________
20. Transesophageal echocardiogram, total service ____________
21. Ear oximetry for O_2 saturation ____________
22. S&I for cardiac cath with angiography ____________
23. Stress echocardiogram, complete ____________
24. Complete ambulatory blood pressure monitoring ____________
25. Electrical testing of blink reflex ____________

Name ____________________

Medicine – III (96100-0183T)

2008 CPT Codes

1. Nurse visit to patient's home for urinary catheter change ____________
2. Poisoning treatment with Ipecac, observation ____________
3. Iontophoresis, 35 minutes ____________
4. Limited developmental testing with report ____________
5. OMT, head and neck ____________
6. IV conscious sedation, 25 minutes, male, age 67 ____________
7. Cryotherapy ablation unilateral renal tumor ____________
8. Acupuncture, 4 needles ____________
9. New patient visit, starred procedure performed ____________
10. DEXA analysis, bilateral hips ____________
11. Telogen/antigen counts on hair clipped at the lab ____________
12. Dexterity testing, hand, 30 minutes, with report ____________
13. Behavior intervention, 30 minutes, twins and both parents ____________
14. Three hours medical testimony ____________
15. Initial visit for newborn born at home ____________
16. Scalpel wound debridement, 14.5 sq. centimeters ____________
17. Reevaluation of physical therapy treatment ____________
18. Diabetic meal planning education, 1 hour, 4 patients ____________
19. Home visit and enema for fecal impaction ____________
20. Patient education/counseling, prescribed beta-blocker medication ____________
21. Chemotherapy. arterial infusion, 55 minutes ____________
22. Gait and stairs retraining, 30 minutes ____________
23. IM chemotherapy administration ____________
24. Chiropractic treatment, 2 spinal areas ____________
25. Two home visit infusions, 5 y/o with hemophilia ____________

HCPCS LEVEL II CODES

Developed by the Health Care Financing Administration (now CMS), HCPCS (Healthcare Common Procedure Coding System) National Level II codes identify nearly 5,000 codes and descriptive terminology for services not included in CPT. HCPCS provides codes for reporting supplies, injectables, and the services of non-physician providers such as ambulance companies and dentists. HCPCS code changes start on January 1 with CPT.

Level II HCPCS codes begin with a letter followed by four digits. Although the codes were originally designed for Medicare and Medicaid, private insurers are beginning to accept and understand them. There were also Level III HCPCS codes. These began with W, X, Y, or Z, and were established by each Medicare carrier. Because of this, Level III codes were excluded from the HCPCS Level II code reference. The standardization of codes sets required by HIPAA eliminated the use of Level III codes in 2003.

HCPCS lists codes alphabetically. Some Level II sections are unusual. K codes are used only by Durable Medical Equipment Regional Carriers (DMERCs) and are temporary codes. Many M (medical) services eventually appear in CPT. Q codes are temporary codes, sometimes appearing mid-year when it becomes necessary to identify a service previously included in or reported by another code. Medicare and Medicaid bulletins will tell you when to report a new Q code.

Read the introduction for an explanation of the HCPCS reference. Each of the sections begins with guidelines on how to use the codes correctly. There may be a mini-index to that section. The HCPCS index may show a single code, a range of codes, or provide no listing for that service. Like the CPT index, you may need to think of other ways to describe the service if you are to find the correct code.

HCPCS modifiers appear in Appendix A or 1. Another Appendix contains a summary of code changes. A different appendix has a list of modified or deleted codes. There are two sorted lists in HCPCS, a table of drugs and a general index. Many private companies print versions of this codebook. Your reference may have numbers or letters to identify each appendix, or differ in format, but the codes and descriptions should be consistent with all vendors. These companies may provide an expanded index or additional information on the use of these codes.

As you code the worksheet, start with the index. Then verify the code(s) with the actual code section, as there may be sizes, quantities, or other variables in selecting the correct code. Read the guidelines to be certain you select the proper code. Many terms are similar and may be unfamiliar. If you use these codes in your work, consult with your employer to be certain you report the correct code.

HCPCS has special alphanumeric or two-letter modifiers. Some of these are included in the Modifier worksheet.

Name ________________________

HCPCS Level II Codes

2008 HCPCS

1. Delivery of monaural behind the ear ____________
2. Medicaid case management, one month ____________
3. Injection, 1.2 million units Bicillin C-R ____________
4. Premolded removable metatarsal support, right foot ____________
5. Chelation therapy ____________
6. In-home occupational therapy, 30 minutes ____________
7. Right shoe modified with outside sole wedge ____________
8. Single root canal, right upper incisor ____________
9. Injection, 8 mg. Compazine ____________
10. Preschool screening for language problems ____________
11. Vinyl urinary bag with tube and leg strap ____________
12. Custom made plastic artificial eye ____________
13. Obtained Pap smear, sent to lab ____________
14. Methotrexate, 50 mg. ____________
15. Non-emergency transportation by wheelchair van ____________
16. Nasogastric tubing, no stylet ____________
17. Adjustable aluminum three prong cane, with tips ____________
18. Non-sterile gloves, one box of 100 ____________
19. Mitomycin, 60 mg. ____________
20. Took x-ray to nursing home, 1 patient seen ____________
21. Hook hand prosthesis, closing ____________
22. Injection, Estradiol, 9 mg. ____________
23. Needleless injection device ____________
24. Toronto orthosis for Legg Perthes ____________
25. Recording apnea monitor, high risk infant ____________

Modifiers

Modifiers are two-character suffixes for procedure codes. They provide important information on how that service changed in some way without altering the definition of the code. Using modifiers properly eliminates some of the need to send procedure notes with claims. All CPT modifiers are two-digit numbers and HCPCS modifiers are two letters or a letter and digit. Some modifiers apply to evaluation and management services only while others clarify surgical procedures. Both CPT and HCPCS list some relevant modifiers within some code sections and provide a complete list of modifiers in an appendix.

CPT modifiers may indicate a reduced or expanded service, bilateral procedures, or the professional component of a service. HCPCS modifiers may indicate the rental or purchase of a piece of equipment, services by a social worker, or that the services were provided in a medically underserved area. Medicare and Medicaid may also direct you to apply HCPCS modifiers to CPT codes. Like the codes they modify, modifiers may be changed or eliminated with each new edition of CPT or HCPCS.

Appendix A shows the modifiers as –22 or –AN. The "–" is not usually reported but is useful if you write out a code as "12345–22" or "54321–LT." The claim form has a special column for modifiers. Some payers may ask you to report modifiers as a five-character code, 09922 or 099LT. The worksheet requires a modifier for each scenario. Use the appendix in the CPT and HCPCS codebooks to select the correct two-character modifier. Some items may require multiple answers.

Name ____________________

Modifiers

2008 CPT

1. The patient had major surgery by Dr. Jones on July 16, and saw the doctor on August 4 for an unrelated office visit. The August 4 service requires modifier: 24
2. Dr. Brown asks Dr. White to assist at a major surgery because a surgery resident is not available. Dr. White reports the surgery code with modifier: 82
3. When an insurer requires a presurgical second opinion, the service is reported with the modifier: 32
4. The surgery was difficult because the patient was a paraplegic weighing 427 pounds. To report these circumstances to the insurer, use modifier: 22
5. Dr. Gray, the family doctor, asks a surgeon, Dr. Green, to see Mrs. Brown at City Hospital, as she may need surgery. Dr. Green schedules the surgery for tomorrow and reports today's service with modifier: 57
6. Dr. Thomas does an appendectomy and removes a mole from the patient's neck while in the OR. Use modifier ___ on the ___ service line of the claim form. 51/(59)

2008 HCPCS

7. Dr. Reed, a clinical psychologist, saw a Medicare patient for diagnostic testing. Dr. Reed reports 96100 with modifier: ________
8. If you refile a claim and change the procedure code because it was incorrect on the original claim, use modifier: ________
9. When a procedure is recorded on an analog tape recorder, use modifier QT. For a digital recording use: ________
10. Dr. Johns owns the portable x-ray equipment, but Dr. Hopkins does the interpretation and report. Identify the modifiers for both doctors: ________
11. Dr. Little sees patients in an inner city clinic, serving in a Physician Scarcity Area. He receives additional compensation for these services by reporting modifier: ________
12. Mr. Small obtains a cane from the medical supply store. If it was a new cane, report modifier: ________

INTRODUCTION TO ICD-9-CM

Diagnosis coding systems are older than procedure coding methods. More than one hundred years ago a French physician developed a system for coding causes of death. In the early 1900s, the U.S. Public Health Service (PHS) began using the same codes. The World Health Organization (WHO) developed ICD-8 in the late 1930s. In 1950, the PHS and the Veterans Administration (VA) adopted ICD-8, the International Classification of Disease, Eighth Revision, Adapted. With the U.S. implementation of ICDA-8 (ICD Adapted), our information on mortality could be matched with statistics from the rest of the world.

Non-governmental hospitals began to use ICDA-8, and the PHS expanded the system to include codes for surgery and treatment. Private agencies were also developing coding structures and by the 1960s the U.S. used at least two diagnosis coding systems. In 1979, the government mandated the use of a new system, ICD-9-CM, for reporting services to Medicare and Medicaid extended to all payers by HIPAA.

The ICD-9-CM, International Classification of Disease, Ninth Revision, Clinical Modification, is compatible with the WHO system, ICD-9. Congress required a standardized coding system for the implementation of DRGs, Diagnosis Related Groups, in 1983. The DRGs are Medicare's hospital payment method. All the diagnoses in ICD-9-CM are grouped into fewer than 500 DRGs. The hospital receives payment for the patient's DRG category, not the cost of the patient's care.

After the government standardized the diagnosis coding system, many private organizations started printing ICD-9-CM with improvements. Some place a color-coded box over the numbers that need a fourth or fifth digit; some distribute the codes in a ring binder; another has anatomical drawings throughout that illustrate the codes. You may buy a loose-leaf subscription for updated pages from some agencies. The government no longer prints an annual edition of ICD-9-CM, and does warn that they are not responsible for the errors made by others in printing the codes.

ICD-9-CM updates codes on a quarterly basis but if the office buys a new book each summer, it should be safe to use for the next year. The publishers usually print the year prominently on the cover so you know when the book becomes obsolete. If the office subscribes to an update service for a loose-leaf ICD-9-CM, remember the October 1st implementation date, as you may not notice if you fail to receive the new pages.

The doctor's office uses two of the three volumes of ICD-9-CM. Volume 1, the Tabular List, provides the codes by body system, in numeric order. Volume 2, the Alphabetic Index, contains many diagnoses that are missing in the Tabular List. After finding the diagnosis in Alphabetic Index, it must be verified with Tabular List. If you use only the Alphabetic Index or only the Tabular List you may select an incorrect code. For convenience, these are frequently printed with the alphabetical index first. Volume 3 of ICD-9-CM contains procedure codes used by hospitals. The doctor's office uses CPT for reporting services, not Volume 3.

Many physicians' offices use only 50 to 100 diagnosis codes. Rather than look them up each time, codes appear on encounter forms or "cheat sheets" used by the billers. There are two problems with this approach. First, the list restricts the number of diagnoses available. Do all the patients have only two or three kinds of hypertension? Second, the office must update the codes on an annual basis. Maybe they review these codes only when they need to order encounter forms. Unfortunately, if you order forms in August, your forms may not have the updated codes required for the next year.

It seems reasonable to assume that with all the updating of codes, we will eventually need a completely new system. ICD-10-CM is coming but the U.S. will delay its implementation until at least the year 2010 or later. The HIPAA mandated changes must be implemented before we can consider ICD-10-CM. Until then, you must become familiar with ICD-9-CM.

Using ICD-9-CM

The office may code either the principal diagnosis or the primary diagnosis for the patient visit. The principal diagnosis is the condition found after study. The primary diagnosis is the reason for the visit. Suppose you see a patient complaining of abdominal pain. If you can establish the cause, such as acute appendicitis, you may report that code. If the complaints are vague, maybe the flu, the threat of layoffs at work, or an upcoming week of final exams, the doctor may code "abdominal pain" for the office visit. Hospitals use the principal diagnosis.

While using CPT, we found very few services described by a person's name, an eponym. A medical term or anatomical description identified most procedures. One exception to this rule is bunion surgery where proper names are used to differentiate surgical techniques, such as Mitchell, Keller, McBride, etc. Diagnoses frequently use a person's name: Parkinson's or Cushing's disease, or a Bennett fracture. This is probably because the diagnosis coding system is older and diseases were traditionally named for the physician first reporting the condition.

As you did with CPT, you will need to become familiar with the coding conventions of ICD-9-CM. The medical office should observe the rules on "includes" and "excludes" but we have limited use for the "code also underlying disease." Before beginning the worksheets, take time to review the introduction, the terminology, and the format of the Tabular and Alphabetic volumes. Some editions of ICD-9-CM are specifically designed for coding in the doctor's office. If you are fortunate enough to have one of those, read all the preliminary information for many helpful hints on using ICD-9-CM.

Diagnosis Coding - Quick and Dirty

Billers receive many invitations to attend seminars on the fine art of diagnosis coding. The instructors are frequently medical records people who must be exact in their hospital reporting. They emphasize accuracy above all else. Unfortunately, it is not that easy in the doctor's office. The diagnosis coding system was developed to collect information worldwide on the presence of disease. We must use the same system to defend charging for medical services. As an example, there are few problems not made worse by obesity. Since obesity is not the problem we are treating, it is not mentioned. If fact, many insurers would not pay for any service billed with the diagnosis of obesity.

Mental health and other programs may authorize a limited number of services and specify the diagnosis code to use for those visits. To be paid, you must report the authorized diagnosis even if the visit concerned other problems.

Also, the doctor's office may be limited to only one diagnosis per service. We simply must select the "best" diagnosis code for the service. Diagnosis codes must be reasonable for the service performed. Always subject your coding to a reasonableness test. The next worksheet will show you how. The answers appear after The Ten Commandments of Diagnosis Coding. The ICD-9-CM Official Guidelines for Coding and Reporting appear after Reasonableness Testing.

Reasonableness Testing

Procedures and diagnoses must be reasonable; they must match each other. No one will declare it reasonable to x-ray a foot for a broken wrist. To assure that your choices come from the correct sections, the summary tables are presented below.

Diagnoses

	Range	Section
1.	001-139	Infectious/Parasitic Disease
2.	140-239	Neoplasms
3.	240-279	Endocrine/Nutrition/Immunity
4.	280-289	Blood/Blood-Forming Organs
5.	290-319	Mental Disorders
6.	320-389	Nervous System/Sense Organs
7.	390-459	Circulatory Systems
8.	460-519	Respiratory System
9.	520-579	Digestive System
10.	580-629	Genitourinary System
11.	630-677	Pregnancy/Childbirth
12.	680-709	Skin/Subcutaneous Tissue
13.	710-739	Musculoskeletal/Connective Tissue
14.	740-759	Congenital Anomalies
15.	760-779	Perinatal Conditions
16.	780-799	Symptoms/Signs/Ill-Defined Conditions
17.	800-999	Injury/Poisoning
18.	V01-V86	Health Status/Contact V-codes
19.	E800-E999	External Causes E-codes

Procedures

	Range	Section
1.	99201-99499	Evaluation/Management
2.	00100-01999	Anesthesia
3.	10021-19499	Integumentary System
4.	20000-29999	Musculoskeletal System
5.	30000-32999	Respiratory System
6.	33010-37799	Cardiovascular System
7.	38100-39599	Hemic/Lymph/Mediastinum
8.	40490-49999	Digestive System
9.	50010-53899	Urinary System
10.	54000-55899	Male Genital System
11.	55970-59899	Intersex/Female/Maternity
12.	60000-64999	Endocrine/Nervous Systems
13.	65091-68899	Eye/Ocular Adnexa
14.	69000-69990	Auditory System
15.	70010-79999	Radiology Services
16.	80047-89356	Pathology Services
17.	90281-99602	Medical Services
18.	0001F-0183T	Category II and III Codes

Using these tables, we can determine "reasonable" coding sections for procedures and diagnoses. If we assume there are no significant complications, we can select the reasonable code ranges for a fractured finger:

Diagnoses: Musculoskeletal (13), Injury (17), External Causes (19)
Procedures: E/M (1), Musculoskeletal (3), Radiology (15)

Using the code section numbers, identify diagnoses and procedures for:

1. Headache: Diagnoses:
   Procedures:
2. Pneumothorax: Diagnoses:
   Procedures:
3. Ulcer: Diagnoses:
   Procedures:

ICD-9-CM Official Guidelines for Coding and Reporting

Effective October 1, 2007. Narrative changes appear in bold text.

Section IV. Diagnostic Coding and Reporting Guidelines for Outpatient Services

These coding guidelines for outpatient diagnoses have been approved for use by hospitals/ providers in coding and reporting hospital-based outpatient services and provider-based office visits.

Information about the use of certain abbreviations, punctuation, symbols, and other conventions used in the ICD-9-CM Tabular List (code numbers and titles) can be found in Section IA of

from ICD-9-CM Official Guidelines for Coding and Reporting
Effective October 1, 2007
Page 87 of 105

these guidelines, under "Conventions Used in the Tabular List." Information about the correct sequence to use in finding a code is also described in Section I.

The terms encounter and visit are often used interchangeably in describing outpatient service contacts and, therefore, appear together in these guidelines without distinguishing one from the other.

Though the conventions and general guidelines apply to all settings, coding guidelines for outpatient and provider reporting of diagnoses will vary in a number of instances from those for inpatient diagnoses, recognizing that:

The Uniform Hospital Discharge Data Set (UHDDS) definition of principal diagnosis applies only to inpatients in acute, short-term, long-term care and psychiatric hospitals.

Coding guidelines for inconclusive diagnoses (probable, suspected, rule out, etc.) were developed for inpatient reporting and do not apply to outpatients.

A. Selection of first-listed condition

In the outpatient setting, the term first-listed diagnosis is used in lieu of principal diagnosis.

In determining the first-listed diagnosis the coding conventions of ICD-9-CM, as well as the general and disease specific guidelines take precedence over the outpatient guidelines.

Diagnoses often are not established at the time of the initial encounter/visit. It may take two or more visits before the diagnosis is confirmed.

The most critical rule involves beginning the search for the correct code assignment through the Alphabetic Index. Never begin searching initially in the Tabular List as this will lead to coding errors.

1. Outpatient Surgery

When a patient presents for outpatient surgery, code the reason for the surgery as the first-listed diagnosis (reason for the encounter), even if the surgery is not performed due to a contraindication.

2. Observation Stay

When a patient is admitted for observation for a medical condition, assign a code for the medical condition as the first-listed diagnosis.

When a patient presents for outpatient surgery and develops complications requiring admission to observation, code the reason for the surgery as the first reported diagnosis (reason for the encounter), followed by codes for the complications as secondary diagnoses.

B. Codes from 001.0 through V84.8

The appropriate code or codes from 001.0 through V84.8 must be used to identify diagnoses, symptoms, conditions, problems, complaints, or other reason(s) for the encounter/visit.

C. Accurate reporting of ICD-9-CM diagnosis codes

For accurate reporting of ICD-9-CM diagnosis codes, the documentation should describe the patient's condition, using terminology which includes specific diagnoses as well as symptoms, problems, or reasons for the encounter. There are ICD-9-CM codes to describe all of these.

D. Selection of codes 001.0 through 999.9

The selection of codes 001.0 through 999.9 will frequently be used to describe the reason for the encounter. These codes are from the section of ICD-9-CM for the classification of diseases and injuries (e.g. infectious and parasitic diseases; neoplasms; symptoms, signs, and ill-defined conditions, etc.).

E. Codes that describe symptoms and signs

Codes that describe symptoms and signs, as opposed to diagnoses, are acceptable for reporting purposes when a diagnosis has not been established (confirmed) by the provider. Chapter 16 of ICD-9-CM, Symptoms, Signs, and Ill-defined conditions (codes 780.0 - 799.9) contain many, but not all codes for symptoms.

F. Encounters for circumstances other than a disease or injury

ICD-9-CM provides codes to deal with encounters for circumstances other than a disease or injury. The Supplementary Classification of factors Influencing Health Status and Contact with Health Services (V01.0- V84.8) is provided to deal with occasions when circumstances other than a disease or injury are recorded as diagnosis or problems. ***See Section I.C. 18 for information on V-codes***

G. Level of Detail in Coding

1. ICD-9-CM codes with 3, 4, or 5 digits

ICD-9-CM is composed of codes with either 3, 4, or 5 digits. Codes with three digits are included in ICD-9-CM as the heading of a category of codes that may be further subdivided by the use of fourth and/or fifth digits, which provide greater specificity.

2. Use of full number of digits required for a code

A three-digit code is to be used only if it is not further subdivided. Where fourth-digit subcategories and/or fifth-digit subclassifications are provided, they must be assigned. A code is invalid if it has not been coded to the full number of digits required for that code.
See also discussion under Section I.b.3., General Coding Guidelines, Level of Detail in Coding.

from ICD-9-CM Official Guidelines for Coding and Reporting
Effective October 1, 2007
Page 89 of 105

H. ICD-9-CM code for the diagnosis, condition, problem, or other reason for encounter/visit

List first the ICD-9-CM code for the diagnosis, condition, problem, or other reason for encounter/visit shown in the medical record to be chiefly responsible for the services provided. List additional codes that describe any coexisting conditions. In some cases the first-listed diagnosis may be a symptom when a diagnosis has not been established (confirmed) by the physician.

I. Uncertain diagnosis

Do not code diagnoses documented as "probable", "suspected," "questionable," "rule out," or "working diagnosis" or other similar terms indicating uncertainty. Rather, code the condition(s) to the highest degree of certainty for that encounter/visit, such as symptoms, signs, abnormal test results, or other reason for the visit.
Please note: This differs from the coding practices used by short-term, acute care, long-term care and psychiatric hospitals.

J. Chronic diseases

Chronic diseases treated on an ongoing basis may be coded and reported as many times as the patient receives treatment and care for the condition(s)

K. Code all documented conditions that coexist

Code all documented conditions that coexist at the time of the encounter/visit, and require or affect patient care treatment or management. Do not code conditions that were previously treated and no longer exist. However, history codes (V10-V19) may be used as secondary codes if the historical condition or family history has an impact on current care or influences treatment.

L. Patients receiving diagnostic services only

For patients receiving diagnostic services only during an encounter/visit, sequence first the diagnosis, condition, problem, or other reason for encounter/visit shown in the medical record to be chiefly responsible for the outpatient services provided during the encounter/visit. Codes for other diagnoses (e.g., chronic conditions) may be sequenced as additional diagnoses.

For encounters for routine laboratory/radiology testing in the absence of any signs, symptoms, or associated diagnosis, assign V72.5 and V72.6. If routine testing is performed during the same encounter as a test to evaluate a sign, symptom, or diagnosis, it is appropriate to assign both the V code and the code describing the reason for the non-routine test.

For outpatient encounters for diagnostic tests that have been interpreted by a physician, and the final report is available at the time of coding, code any confirmed or definitive diagnosis(es) documented in the interpretation. Do not code related signs and symptoms as additional diagnoses.

from ICD-9-CM Official Guidelines for Coding and Reporting
Effective October 1, 2007
Page 90 of 105

Please note: This differs from the coding practice in the hospital inpatient setting regarding abnormal findings on test results.

M. Patients receiving therapeutic services only

For patients receiving therapeutic services only during an encounter/visit, sequence first the diagnosis, condition, problem, or other reason for encounter/visit shown in the medical record to be chiefly responsible for the outpatient services provided during the encounter/visit. Codes for other diagnoses (e.g., chronic conditions) may be sequenced as additional diagnoses.

The only exception to this rule is that when the primary reason for the admission/encounter is chemotherapy, radiation therapy, or rehabilitation, the appropriate V code for the service is listed first, and the diagnosis or problem for which the service is being performed listed second.

N. Patients receiving preoperative evaluations only

For patients receiving preoperative evaluations only, sequence first a code from category V72.8, Other specified examinations, to describe the pre-op consultations. Assign a code for the condition to describe the reason for the surgery as an additional diagnosis. Code also any findings related to the pre-op evaluation.

O. Ambulatory surgery

For ambulatory surgery, code the diagnosis for which the surgery was performed. If the postoperative diagnosis is known to be different from the preoperative diagnosis at the time the diagnosis is confirmed, select the postoperative diagnosis for coding, since it is the most definitive.

P. Routine outpatient prenatal visits

For routine outpatient prenatal visits when no complications are present, codes V22.0, Supervision of normal first pregnancy, or V22.1, Supervision of other normal pregnancy, should be used as the principal diagnosis. These codes should not be used in conjunction with chapter 11 codes.

The Ten Commandments of Diagnosis Coding

An irreverent summary of rules with practical coding hints

I. The largest number of digits wins.

Do not report three if there are four, do not report four if there are five.

II. Numeric codes win over alphanumeric.

If the condition is listed twice, once with a letter and once with all numbers, use the one with all numbers, if possible.

III. Watch out for punctuation.

Do not even think it. Do not think "427 point 0" or "250 point 00." These codes are 4270 and 25000. Many claim form scanners and electronic claim programs cannot process the punctuation mark correctly.

IV. Use only the code(s) related to the services performed.

A patient with acute bronchitis and heart disease is seen for the bronchitis. The chart indicates it is time for an ECG. If you code the ECG for bronchitis, it may not pay. With Medicare, it could result in a "not medically necessary" rejection.

V. Diagnosis coding does not raise the payment, only allows it.

A "better" diagnosis will not raise the payment. The neck can be x-rayed for pain, arthritis, or cervical fracture: all will allow payment. The diagnosis of foot pain, even if treated at this office visit, does not justify a neck x-ray.

VI. Do not code in greater specificity than the information provided.

Do not code "rule out" and "suspected" as if the condition existed. The patient is seen because she thinks she broke her hand. If related to an accident and when the x-ray does not confirm a fracture, code "pain" or "contusion" or "traumatic injury."

VII. Neoplasms are always benign, unless stated to be malignant. If malignant, they are always primary, unless stated to be secondary or in situ.

Some lesion codes are general, others are found in the neoplasm table. When using the table, be certain to select the correct column and verify that code with the Tabular List. Do not give the patient something he does not have, and cannot be documented as treated.

VIII. Always verify codes selected from the Alphabetic Index with the Tabular List.

IX. Diagnosis codes in the Tabular List, in italics, cannot be used as the primary diagnosis.

These codes are listed as "excludes" or "code also the underlying disease." Be certain the correct code is selected and verified.

X. Sometimes the best diagnosis code is going to be the one that is least incorrect.

Diagnosis Coding Worksheet Instructions

This workbook divides ICD-9-CM into sections, each with two worksheets. Exercise I requires the use of the Tabular List. Study the code section of the Tabular List and record the appropriate THREE-DIGIT category indicator for where you would find that condition listed. Your search may be easier if you look in the ICD-9-CM Appendix E for the three-digit categories. Then go to the Tabular section for verification of your choice. Always read the introductory notes at the beginning of each section to find the basic rules for the codes in that category.

The second exercise requires a search of the Alphabetic Index and verification of the code in the Tabular volume. Some diagnosis codes require a fifth digit that may not be easy to find in the Alphabetic Index.

Take the time to look around the reference volumes as you use them. Some of the worksheet codes have very unusual codes listed near them. Would you believe there is a diagnosis called "no room at the inn"? Can you guess what it means? Look it up and see if you were right.

Answers to the Reasonableness Test:

1. Diagnosis: 5, 6, 7, 8, 13, 16
   Procedure: 1, 4, 11, 12, 13, 15, 17
2. Diagnosis: 8, 16, 17
   Procedure: 1, 5, 15, 16, 17
3. Gotcha! There isn't enough information here to code this one correctly. Is it a skin ulcer, mouth ulcer, or abdominal ulcer? Identify all the ulcer types you can think of, and code them all for diagnoses and procedures.

Name ______________________

Infectious/Parasitic Diseases - I (001-139)

2008 ICD-9-CM

These diseases are generally considered communicable or transmissible. Also included are a few diseases of unknown or possibly infectious origin. You must use caution with these codes, as they can affect employment possibilities, such as identifying a communicable disease for a food handler, a cook, or a waiter. A person's ability to obtain life or health insurance can be affected by a report of one of these diseases, and there could be other significant consequences. This section contains the codes for AIDS, ARC, and HIV used to register patients with the Centers for Disease Control and Prevention (CDC).

Additionally, an incorrectly reported diagnosis can indicate that a condition was diagnosed but never treated. There would be no documentation supporting referral or therapy for the misdiagnosis. This could also raise malpractice issues of failure to treat or abandonment.

Using the Tabular List only, identify the three-digit category for:

1. Salmonella ____________
2. Hepatitis ____________
3. Late effects of polio ____________
4. TB of central nervous system ____________
5. Herpes simplex ____________
6. Mumps ____________
7. Trench mouth ____________
8. HIV with Kaposi's Sarcoma ____________
9. Gangrene ____________
10. Warts ____________

Name ____________________

Infectious/Parasitic Diseases - II (001-139)

Using the alphabetic and/or tabular references, locate the following diseases and code to acceptable specificity, three, four, or five characters.

1. Acute viral conjunctivitis with hemorrhage ____________
2. Death from bite of wild dog ____________
3. Seven day Queensland fever ____________
4. Lyme disease ____________
5. Ringworm ____________
6. Trichomonal fluor ____________
7. Congenital syphilitic osteomyelitis ____________
8. *e. coli* intestinal infection ____________
9. Dandy fever ____________
10. Ground itch ____________
11. Hiss-Russell shigellosis ____________
12. Haverhill streptobacillus ____________
13. Pseudocowpox ____________
14. Subacute spongiform encephalopathy ____________
15. Paratyphoid fever ____________
16. Rubella encephalitis ____________
17. Australian X disease ____________
18. Pulmonary paracoccidioidomycosis ____________
19. Intestinal tuberculosis found in sputum ____________
20. Schaumann's lymphogranulomatosis ____________
21. Early macular leprosy ____________
22. Lupus tuberculosis ____________
23. Herpetic felon ____________
24. African eyeworm infection ____________
25. Monkey malaria ____________

Name ________________________

Neoplasms - I (140-239)

2008 ICD-9-CM

Coders frequently have trouble with neoplasms. Accuracy is critical if the doctor plans to enroll the patient in one of the cancer registry services. A Johns-Hopkins representative told of finding that over 50% of the patients in their tumor registry did not have the cancer specified in their enrollment records. Referring physician errors on the registration documents caused Johns-Hopkins to send the doctors information on treating the wrong kind of tumor.

Read the instructions for this section very carefully. The Alphabetic Index contains a neoplasm table. This is the starting place when you look for a neoplasm code. The table has a separate code for primary, secondary, and CA in situ. The Tabular List arranges the codes by body site, in a similar sequence as the neoplasm table. As a general practice, avoid coding "uncertain behavior" and "unspecified." Try to hold any claim until you know the type of neoplasm. If you code malignant, and it is benign, it may be very difficult to get the records changed. If you code benign and it is malignant, you may not receive the correct payment.

Caution: There is a "trick" question on the worksheet. Read the instructions carefully!

Using the Tabular List only, identify the three-digit category for:

1. Malignant neoplasm of tongue ____________
2. Benign neoplasm of tongue ____________
3. Skin carcinoma in situ ____________
4. Leukemia ____________
5. Malignant neoplasm of pancreas ____________
6. Kaposi's Sarcoma ____________
7. Breast carcinoma in situ ____________
8. Neoplasm, nature unknown ____________
9. Lung malignancy ____________
10. Bladder cancer ____________

Name ________________________

Neoplasms - II (140-239)

Using the alphabetic and/or tabular references, locate the following diseases and code to acceptable specificity, three, four, or five characters.

1. Ventriculi carcinoma ____________
2. Primary cancer of the cauda equina ____________
3. Tumor of the lip ____________
4. Carcinoma in situ, thalamus ____________
5. Tumor of coccyx, secondary to brain cancer ____________
6. Neurofibroma, abdominal wall skin ____________
7. Cancer of the brain ____________
8. Metastasis to Zuckerkandl's organ ____________
9. Unspecified tumor of Cowper's gland ____________
10. Benign tumor of the left eyebrow ____________
11. Metastatic carcinoma of the omentum ____________
12. Uterine malignancy ____________
13. Benign neoplasm renal pelvis ____________
14. Polycythemia vera ____________
15. Mesocolonic malignancy ____________
16. Pancreatic glucagonoma ____________
17. Lymphangioendothelioma ____________
18. Malignant neoplasm of submaxillary gland ____________
19. Tracheal carcinoma in situ ____________
20. Benign tumor of thymus ____________
21. Non-Hodgkin's lymphoma ____________
22. Benign tumor of breast, male ____________
23. Cancer of the respiratory system ____________
24. Retrobulbar malignancy, left eye ____________
25. Glossopalatine fold carcinoma ____________

Name ____________________

Endocrine, Nutritional, Metabolic, Immunity Disorders - I (240-279)

2008 ICD-9-CM

This section deals with diseases NOT caused by tumor. These are some of the most common reasons for a visit to the doctor's office. Many of these conditions are hereditary, many last a lifetime. Many contribute to health complications as we age. As a wise man once said, "Most people die of the cumulative effects of heredity, lifestyle, and environment."

Using the Tabular List only, identify the three-digit category for:

1. Hyperlipidemia ____________
2. Diabetes ____________
3. Thyrotoxicosis ____________
4. Vitamin D deficiency ____________
5. Dwarfism ____________
6. Obesity ____________
7. Beriberi ____________
8. Testicular dysfunction ____________
9. Acute thyroid disease ____________
10. Gout ____________

Name ____________________

Endocrine, Nutritional, Metabolic, Immunity Disorders - II (240-279)

Using the alphabetic and/or tabular references, locate the following diseases and code to acceptable specificity, three, four, or five characters.

1. Proliferative diabetic retinopathy ____________
2. Addison's disease ____________
3. Xylulosuria ____________
4. Pickwickian syndrome ____________
5. Glucoglycinuria ____________
6. Hashimoto's disease ____________
7. Diabetic coma ____________
8. Lymphatism ____________
9. Graves' disease ____________
10. Pendred's syndrome ____________
11. Severe malnutrition from dieting ____________
12. Forbes-Albright syndrome ____________
13. Pseudopseudohypoparathyroidism ____________
14. Iatrogenic hyperinsulinism ____________
15. Nezelof's syndrome ____________
16. Adenomatous thyroid cyst with storm ____________
17. Mild malnutrition ____________
18. Urbach-Wiethe syndrome ____________
19. Sporadic goitrous cretinism ____________
20. Uric acid nephrolithiasis ____________
21. Respiratory alkalosis ____________
22. Alcoholic pellagra ____________
23. Struma nodosa ____________
24. Night blindness due to vitamin deficiency ____________
25. Acute rickets ____________

Name ______________________

Blood and Blood-Forming Organs - I (280-289)

2008 ICD-9-CM

This section covers diseases of the blood and blood-forming organs. Anemia and clotting disorders are the most common.

Using the Tabular List only, identify the three-digit category for:

1. Christmas disease ____________
2. Cooley's anemia ____________
3. Infantile pseudoleukemia ____________
4. Marchiafava-Micheli syndrome ____________
5. Imerslund's syndrome ____________
6. Aplastic anemia NOS ____________
7. Hereditary hyposegmentation ____________
8. Sideropenic dysphagia ____________
9. Emotional polycythemia ____________
10. Megakaryocytic hypoplasia ____________

Name ______________________

Blood and Blood-Forming Organs - II (280-289)

Using the alphabetic and/or tabular references, locate the following diseases and code to acceptable specificity, three, four, or five characters.

1. Antithromboplastinemia ____________
2. Paroxysmal cold disease ____________
3. Massive blood transfusion thrombocytopenia ____________
4. Lipophagocytosis ____________
5. Impoverished blood ____________
6. Siderotic splenomegaly ____________
7. Chronic Hemoglobin S disease ____________
8. Plummer-Vinson disease ____________
9. Autoimmune cold sensitivity ____________
10. Iron deficiency anemia ____________
11. Blood dyscrasia ____________
12. Lederer-Brill syndrome ____________
13. Vitamin K deficiency ____________
14. Lazy leukocyte syndrome ____________
15. Classical hemophilia ____________
16. Zurich hemoglobin disease ____________
17. Splenic hyperemia ____________
18. Sclerothymic hyperviscosity syndrome ____________
19. Idiopathic allergic eosinophilia ____________
20. Thrombocytopathy ____________
21. Thalassemic variants ____________
22. Blackfan-Diamond syndrome ____________
23. Hypoleukia splenica ____________
24. Consumption coagulopathy ____________
25. Goat's milk anemia ____________

Name ______________________

Mental Disorders - I (290-319)

2008 ICD-9-CM

Read the introduction carefully. Notice the exclusion of diseases with an organic origin. This section includes psychoses, neuroses, conduct disorders, and retardation.

Caution: Worksheet item 20 on the next page.

Using the Tabular List only, identify the three-digit category for:

1. Neurasthenia ____________
2. Senile dementia ____________
3. Paranoia ____________
4. Voyeurism ____________
5. Anorexia nervosa ____________
6. Schizophrenia ____________
7. Pyromania ____________
8. Dipsomania ____________
9. Dyslexia ____________
10. Delirium tremens ____________

Name ____________________

Mental Disorders - II (290-319)

Using the alphabetic and/or tabular references, locate the following diseases and code to acceptable specificity, three, four, or five characters.

1. Hypochondriac ____________
2. Organic brain syndrome ____________
3. Panic agoraphobia ____________
4. Korsakoff's alcoholic psychosis ____________
5. Munchausen's syndrome ____________
6. Catatonic schizophrenia in remission ____________
7. Pseudocyesis ____________
8. IQ 27 ____________
9. Psychogenic polyarthralgia ____________
10. Megalomania ____________
11. Hyperactive attention deficit disorder ____________
12. Inherited idiocy ____________
13. Huntington's dementia ____________
14. Manic depressive disorder ____________
15. Drug withdrawal syndrome ____________
16. Rare emotional insomnia ____________
17. Asexual trans-sexualism ____________
18. Occasional cocaine abuse ____________
19. Acute chronic paranoid schizophrenia ____________
20. Frequent leader of 4th grade truancy group ____________
21. Shoe fetish ____________
22. Dyspraxic syndrome ____________
23. Psychogenic dyspareunia ____________
24. Subacute infective psychosis ____________
25. Active Heller's syndrome ____________

Name ______________________

Nervous System and Sense Organs - I (320-389)

2008 ICD-9-CM

Inflammatory, hereditary, and degenerative diseases of the central nervous system, as well as disorders of the peripheral nervous system, eyes, and ears are included in this section. Review the table describing the levels of visual impairment and note the difference in the U.S. and WHO definitions of blindness.

Caution: One two-word description may give you different codes depending on which word you look up in the alphabetic index. Both are correct. Isn't that interesting?

Using the Tabular List only, identify the three-digit category for:

1. Hemophilus meningitis ____________
2. Pick's disease ____________
3. Jacksonian epilepsy ____________
4. Pseudocyst of the retina ____________
5. Double vision ____________
6. Otitis media ____________
7. Restless legs ____________
8. Meniere's disease ____________
9. Keratoconus ____________
10. Tic douloureux ____________

Name ______________________

Nervous System and Sense Organs - II (320-389)

Using the alphabetic and/or tabular reference, locate the following diseases and code to acceptable specificity, three, four, or five characters.

1. Retrolental fibroplasia ____________
2. Pseudomonas aeruginosa meningitis ____________
3. Friedreich's ataxia ____________
4. Spastic ophthalmic artery ____________
5. Late effect of subdural brain abscess ____________
6. Hereditary degenerative keratopathy ____________
7. Mastoid cholesteatoma ____________
8. Familial intention tremor ____________
9. Arcus senilis ____________
10. Multiple sclerosis ____________
11. Guillain-Barre syndrome ____________
12. Vitreous floaters ____________
13. Jamaican neuropathy ____________
14. Amaurosis ____________
15. Morton's neuroma ____________
16. Decreased ocular pressure with papilledema ____________
17. Profound blindness both eyes ____________
18. Romberg's syndrome ____________
19. Brain marasmus ____________
20. Irritation 5th cranial nerve ____________
21. Pseudohole of the macula ____________
22. Tympanosclerosis ____________
23. Pars planitis ____________
24. Crossed eyes, alternating A pattern ____________
25. Soemmering's ring ____________

Name ____________________

Circulatory System - I (390-459)

2008 ICD-9-CM

This system includes rheumatic fever and resulting heart disease, hypertensive and ischemic heart disease, diseases of the pulmonary circulation, and other heart diseases. It also includes cerebrovascular disease and diseases of the blood vessels and lymphatics.

Using the Tabular List only, identify the three-digit category for:

1. Aortic insufficiency ____________
2. Ruptured abdominal aortic aneurysm ____________
3. Myocardiopathy ____________
4. Mobitz II block ____________
5. Elephantiasis ____________
6. Postphlebitic syndrome ____________
7. Capillary hemorrhage ____________
8. Buerger's disease ____________
9. Arteriosclerosis ____________
10. Thrombosed hemorrhoids ____________

Name ____________________

Circulatory System - II (390-459)

Using the alphabetic and/or tabular references, locate the following diseases and code to acceptable specificity, three, four, or five characters.

1. Sick sinus syndrome ____________
2. Anterolateral myocardial infarct ____________
3. Kawasaki disease ____________
4. Subacute bacterial endocarditis ____________
5. Congestive failure with malignant hypertension ____________
6. Ruptured berry aneurysm ____________
7. Bifascicular block ____________
8. Temporal arteritis ____________
9. Acute rheumatic endocarditis ____________
10. Bilateral stenosis of carotid artery ____________
11. Superior vena cava syndrome ____________
12. Iliac vein phlebitis ____________
13. Rare African cardiomyopathy ____________
14. Benign renovascular hypertension ____________
15. Atrial flutter ____________
16. Paroxysmal atrial tachycardia ____________
17. Subclavian steal syndrome ____________
18. Transient ischemic attacks ____________
19. Infected stasis ulcers ____________
20. Cerebrovascular insult ____________
21. Nonfilarial chylocele ____________
22. Intermittent claudication ____________
23. Wolff-Parkinson-White disorder ____________
24. Atherosclerosis of coronary artery bypass graft ____________
25. Prinzmetal angina ____________

Name ______________________

Respiratory System - I (460-519)

2008 ICD-9-CM

This system includes acute infections and other respiratory diseases such as pneumonia and influenza, obstructive pulmonary disease, and external causes of lung disease, as well as other forms of lung disorders.

Using the Tabular List only, identify the three-digit category for:

1. Hay fever ____________
2. Hemothorax ____________
3. Detergent asthma ____________
4. Smoker's cough ____________
5. Laryngitis ____________
6. Pleurobronchopneumonia ____________
7. Mediastinitis ____________
8. Pigeon fanciers' disease ____________
9. Sinus polyp ____________
10. Hemophilus pneumonia ____________

Name ______________________

Respiratory System - II (460-519)

Using the alphabetic and/or tabular references, locate the following diseases and code to acceptable specificity, three, four, or five characters.

1. Aspiration pneumonia ____________
2. Traumatic nasal septal deflection ____________
3. Idiopathic diffuse interstitial fibrosis ____________
4. Retropharyngeal abscess ____________
5. Broncholithiasis ____________
6. Acute sinus infection ____________
7. Cork handlers' disease ____________
8. Tracheostenosis ____________
9. Postoperative pulmonary edema ____________
10. Croup ____________
11. Allergic rhinitis ____________
12. Radiation fibrosis of the lung ____________
13. *e. coli* pneumonia ____________
14. Laryngeal muscle spasm ____________
15. Black lung disease ____________
16. Eosinophilic asthma ____________
17. Gangrenous pharyngitis ____________
18. Chronic obstructive pulmonary disease ____________
19. Acute follicular tonsillitis ____________
20. Acute fistular empyema ____________
21. Legionnaire's disease ____________
22. Bullous emphysema ____________
23. Nasopharyngeal inflammation ____________
24. Chlamydia pneumonia ____________
25. Asthmatic bronchitis ____________

Name ________________________

Digestive System - I (520-579)

2008 ICD-9-CM

This unit covers diseases of the oral cavity, salivary glands and jaws, esophagus, stomach and duodenum, appendicitis, abdominal hernias, noninfectious enteritis and colitis, and other diseases of the intestines, peritoneum, and digestive system.

Using the Tabular List only, identify the three-digit category for:

1. Alcoholic cirrhosis ____________
2. Impacted wisdom tooth ____________
3. Cholecystitis ____________
4. Duodenal ulcer ____________
5. Sprue ____________
6. Pyloric stenosis ____________
7. Sialolithiasis ____________
8. Crohn's disease ____________
9. Pancreatitis ____________
10. Peritonitis ____________

Name ____________________

Digestive System - II (520-579)

Using the alphabetic and/or tabular reference, locate the following diseases and code to acceptable specificity, three, four, or five characters.

1. Hematemesis ____________
2. Choledochoduodenal fistula ____________
3. Portal thrombophlebitis ____________
4. Pain in right TMJ ____________
5. Lingua villosa nigra ____________
6. Appendicitis with abscess ____________
7. Postgastrectomy diarrhea ____________
8. Hemorrhagic pancreatitis ____________
9. Acute pyloric ulcer with hemorrhage ____________
10. Melena ____________
11. Recurrent gangrenous inguinal hernia ____________
12. Tooth discoloration from silver fillings ____________
13. Toxic parotitis ____________
14. Malabsorption syndrome ____________
15. Sialodocholithiasis ____________
16. Diverticulosis ____________
17. Intraoral nasolabial cyst ____________
18. Strangulated bowel ____________
19. Strawberry disease of the gallbladder ____________
20. Functional vomiting ____________
21. Retrocecal abscess ____________
22. Crohn’s intestinal disease ____________
23. Gastritis due to alcoholism ____________
24. Intussusception of appendix ____________
25. Chronic appendicitis ____________

Name ______________________

Genitourinary System - I (580-629)

2008 ICD-9-CM

This system includes diseases of the kidneys, bladder, ureter, urethra, and male genital organs. Also covered are the diseases of the breast, inflammatory conditions of the female pelvic organs, and female infertility.

Caution: Item 15 on the next page may be a challenge.

Using the Tabular List only, identify the three-digit category for:

1. Renal failure ____________
2. Kidney stone ____________
3. Acute prostatitis ____________
4. Fibrocystic breast ____________
5. Polymenorrhea ____________
6. Benign prostatic hypertrophy ____________
7. Endometriosis ____________
8. Female infertility ____________
9. Male infertility ____________
10. Phimosis (congenital) ____________

Name ____________________________

Genitourinary System - II (580-629)

Using the alphabetic and/or tabular references, locate the following diseases and code to acceptable specificity, three, four, or five characters.

1. Urinary tract infection (UTI) ____________
2. Post-hysterectomy vaginal prolapse ____________
3. Gynecomastia ____________
4. Penile kraurosis ____________
5. Infertility from low sperm count ____________
6. Salpingo-oophoritis ____________
7. Acute pelvic inflammatory disease ____________
8. Boil of the scrotum ____________
9. Rectovaginal endometriosis ____________
10. Breast lump ____________
11. Bartholin's gland infection ____________
12. Chronic renal failure ____________
13. Cervical erosion ____________
14. Nephropathy NOS ____________
15. Suppurative orchitis ____________
16. Membranoproliferative glomerulonephritis ____________
17. Floating kidney ____________
18. Recurrent urinary fistula ____________
19. Chocolate cyst of the ovary ____________
20. Pelvic congestive disease ____________
21. Balanitis obliterans ____________
22. Senile atrophic vaginitis ____________
23. Anovulatory infertility ____________
24. Subacute nonsuppurative nephritis ____________
25. Rupture of corpus luteum cyst ____________

Name ________________________

Pregnancy, Childbirth, Puerperium - I (630-677)

2008 ICD-9-CM

This unit includes conditions related to ectopic and molar pregnancy, abortive pregnancies, other pregnancy complications; normal delivery, other indications for pregnancy care, and labor and delivery, as well as complications of labor and delivery.

Caution: This is a complicated section. All worksheet II terms must be checked with the Tabular List. Many codes have a required fifth digit. Note the limited options for the fifth digit.

Using the Tabular List only, identify the three-digit category for:

1. Hemorrhoids from pregnancy ____________
2. ABO isoimmunization ____________
3. Ovarian pregnancy ____________
4. Hyperemesis gravidarum ____________
5. Fetopelvic disproportion ____________
6. Cord prolapse ____________
7. Transient hypertension of pregnancy ____________
8. Uterine rupture during labor ____________
9. Twin pregnancy ____________
10. Illegally induced abortion ____________

Name ________________________

Pregnancy, Childbirth, Puerperium - II (630-677)

Using the alphabetic and/or tabular references, locate the following diseases and code to acceptable specificity, three, four, or five characters.

1. Severe antepartum thrombophlebitis ____________
2. Early separation of the placenta ____________
3. Incomplete spontaneous abortion with shock ____________
4. Toxemia with convulsions ____________
5. Delivery of sextuplets ____________
6. Suppressed lactation ____________
7. Reopening of C-section wound ____________
8. Obstetric shock ____________
9. Cardiac arrest from anesthesia for delivery ____________
10. Failed attempted abortion with hemorrhage ____________
11. Postpartum hemorrhage from retained placenta ____________
12. Ruptured fallopian tubal pregnancy ____________
13. Prenatal gestational edema ____________
14. Gonorrhea, 7th month of pregnancy ____________
15. Vaginal hematoma from delivery ____________
16. Benign essential hypertension of pregnancy ____________
17. Antepartum nephritis ____________
18. Cephalopelvic disproportion ____________
19. Threatened abortion ____________
20. Delivery of fetal death in utero ____________
21. Labor complicated by septicemia ____________
22. Missed abortion ____________
23. Spontaneous breech delivery ____________
24. Nursing mother mastitis ____________
25. Renal shutdown following elective pregnancy termination ____________

Name ______________________

Skin and Subcutaneous Tissue - I (680-709)

2008 ICD-9-CM

This section includes infections of the skin and subcutaneous tissue, inflammatory conditions, and other diseases of the skin and subcutaneous tissue.

Using the Tabular List only, identify the three-digit category for:

1. Pressure ulcer ____________
2. Facial boil ____________
3. Ocular pemphigus ____________
4. Paronychia of finger ____________
5. Infected ingrown toenail ____________
6. Poison ivy ____________
7. Baldness ____________
8. Axillary abscess ____________
9. Cafe au lait spots ____________
10. Psoriasis ____________

Name ____________________

Skin and Subcutaneous Tissue - II (680-709)

Using the alphabetic and/or tabular references, locate the following diseases and code to acceptable specificity, three, four, or five characters.

1. Dermatitis due to alcohol ingestion ____________
2. Nail horn, left thumb ____________
3. Lichen-type eruption of axilla ____________
4. Hives from allergy to trees ____________
5. Wilson-Brocq disease ____________
6. Erythema multiforme ____________
7. Rhus ____________
8. Cheloid scar ____________
9. Furunculosis, left temple ____________
10. Asteatosis cutis ____________
11. Polymorphous eruption from tanning booth ____________
12. Infected corn, right foot ____________
13. Alligator skin, recent onset ____________
14. Senile dermatosis ____________
15. Diaper rash ____________
16. Granuloma pyogenicum ____________
17. Hutchinson's cheiropompholyx ____________
18. Solar photosensitivity ____________
19. Gibert's disease ____________
20. Angioma serpiginosum ____________
21. Impetiginous dermatitis ____________
22. Abscess both cheeks and chin ____________
23. Dermatitis from contact with gold ring ____________
24. Chronic neurogenic skin ulcer ____________
25. Miliaria rubra tropicalis ____________

Name ______________________

Musculoskeletal System and Connective Tissue - I (710-739)

2008 ICD-9-CM

This section includes arthropathies and related disorders, dorsopathies, rheumatism (excluding the back), chondropathies, and acquired musculoskeletal deformities. Many codes have a fifth digit. Note that this section excludes fractures.

If you enjoyed coding the musculoskeletal CPT section, you will find this section is even more pleasant. Read very carefully and code only when you are certain of the answer.

Caution: These are large coding lists. You may need information from a previous ICD-9-CM page.

Using the Tabular List only, identify the three-digit category for:

1. Rheumatoid arthritis ____________
2. Lumbago ____________
3. Knee mice ____________
4. Dupuytren's contracture ____________
5. Cauliflower ear ____________
6. Disseminated lupus erythematosus ____________
7. Polymyalgia rheumatica ____________
8. Kyphoscoliosis ____________
9. Kissing spine ____________
10. Hypertrophic pulmonary osteoarthropathy ____________

Name ______________________

Musculoskeletal System and Connective Tissue - II (710-739)

Using the alphabetic and/or tabular references, locate the following diseases and code to acceptable specificity, three, four, or five characters.

1. Achilles tenosynovitis ____________
2. Degenerative polyarticular arthritis ____________
3. Chondromalacia of the patella ____________
4. Tennis elbow ____________
5. Wasting amyotrophy ____________
6. Degenerative joint disease of the spine ____________
7. Staphylococcal pyogenic arthritis ____________
8. Cervical radiculopathy ____________
9. Old bucket handle tear, lateral meniscus ____________
10. Swelling in wrist joint ____________
11. Lordosis following laminectomy ____________
12. Right plantar fasciitis ____________
13. Pyomyositis ossificans ____________
14. Severe bone infection ____________
15. Calcification of lumbar disc ____________
16. Pigeon toes ____________
17. Torticollis ____________
18. Pectus excavatum, acquired ____________
19. Post polio foot drop ____________
20. Flat feet ____________
21. Bowlegs ____________
22. Humpback from old age ____________
23. Low back pain ____________
24. Kaschin-Beck disease, right ankle ____________
25. Spontaneous shoulder muscle rupture ____________

Name ____________________

Congenital Anomalies - I (740-759)

2008 ICD-9-CM

This section contains conditions that people inherit. These codes differentiate congenital heart disease from acquired heart disease.

Using the Tabular List only, identify the three-digit category for:

1. Anophthalmos ____________
2. Port wine stain ____________
3. Congenital pectus excavatum ____________
4. Bicornuate uterus ____________
5. Missing ear on right ____________
6. Klinefelter's syndrome ____________
7. Ventricular septal defect ____________
8. Cleft lip ____________
9. Congenital hip deformity ____________
10. Pyloric stenosis ____________

Name ______________________

Congenital Anomalies - II (740-759)

Using the alphabetic and/or tabular references, locate the following diseases and code to acceptable specificity, three, four, or five characters.

1. Aphalangia, left foot ____________
2. Myelomeningocele ____________
3. Macrodactylism, right thumb ____________
4. Cauda equina developmental defect ____________
5. Congenital displacement of the spleen ____________
6. Cyst of the thyroglossal duct ____________
7. Alligator skin disease ____________
8. True dextrocardia ____________
9. Postductal coarctation of the aorta ____________
10. Achondroplastic dwarf ____________
11. Cryptorchism ____________
12. Endocardial cushion defect ____________
13. Middle ear congenital deformity ____________
14. Premature fontanel ossification ____________
15. Trisomy 21 ____________
16. Autosomal dominant polycystic kidney disease ____________
17. Congenital heart block ____________
18. Block-Sulzberger melanoblastosis ____________
19. Fibular hemimelia ____________
20. Ruysch's disease ____________
21. Gillespie's syndrome ____________
22. Supranumery first rib ____________
23. Ambisexuality ____________
24. Amyotrophia congenita ____________
25. Cleft nose ____________

Name ________________________

Conditions of the Perinatal Period - I (760-779)

2008 ICD-9-CM

This unit covers conditions of the perinatal period and may involve both the mother and fetus or infant.

Caution: Item 16 on the next page may be easier to find using the Tabular List.

Using the Tabular List only, identify the three-digit category for:

1. Maternal death ________
2. Prematurity hyperbilirubinemia ________
3. Exceptionally large baby ________
4. Newborn thrush ________
5. Small for dates ________
6. Newborn seizures ________
7. Fractured clavicle from birthing ________
8. Fetal death from labor anoxia ________
9. "Infant of diabetic mother" syndrome ________
10. Placenta previa ________

Name ____________________________

Conditions of the Perinatal Period - II (760-779)

Using the alphabetic and/or tabular reference, locate the following diseases and code to acceptable specificity, three, four, or five characters.

1. Umbilical cord necrosis ____________
2. Petechiae of newborn infant ____________
3. Fetal listeriosis ____________
4. Accidental birth ____________
5. Newborn transitory tachypnea ____________
6. Premature delivery of 730 gm. infant ____________
7. Drug dependence affecting newborn ____________
8. Facial nerve injury of newborn ____________
9. Prolonged labor affecting fetus ____________
10. Fetal death from pregnancy termination ____________
11. Hyaline membrane disease ____________
12. Newborn delay in meconium passage ____________
13. Fetal alcohol syndrome ____________
14. Unstable lie during pregnancy ____________
15. ABO erythroblastosis ____________
16. Fetal chignon ____________
17. Stillborn ____________
18. Congenital hydrocele ____________
19. Poor fetal growth ____________
20. Hydrops fetalis ____________
21. Mild newborn asphyxia ____________
22. Fetal blood loss from cord hemorrhage ____________
23. Newborn hepatitis ____________
24. Premature infant anemia ____________
25. Exchange transfusion thrombocytopenia ____________

Name ____________________

Symptoms, Signs, and Ill-Defined Conditions - I (780-799)

2008 ICD-9-CM

This section contains codes useful to almost every practice. When you don't know what else to call it, look at coding the symptoms or the signs of the illness or injury that brought the patient to the office.

Using the Tabular List only, identify the three-digit category for:

1. Cardiorespiratory failure ____________
2. Hoarseness ____________
3. Anorexia ____________
4. Old age ____________
5. Cardiogenic shock ____________
6. Abnormal EEG ____________
7. Apnea ____________
8. Carpopedal spasm ____________
9. Waterbrash ____________
10. Abdominal cramps ____________

Name ________________________

Symptoms, Signs, and Ill-Defined Conditions - II (780-799)

Using the alphabetic and/or tabular references, locate the following diseases and code to acceptable specificity, three, four, or five characters.

1. Occult blood in feces ____________
2. Headache ____________
3. Sudden infant death syndrome (SIDS) ____________
4. Transient hypotension ____________
5. Belching ____________
6. Intermittent staggering gait ____________
7. Heart pain ____________
8. Male stress and urge incontinence ____________
9. Acetone in urine ____________
10. Found dead ____________
11. Abnormal blushing ____________
12. Swollen glands ____________
13. Excessive weight gain ____________
14. Abnormal weight loss ____________
15. Positive TB test ____________
16. Nervous tension ____________
17. Vertigo ____________
18. Enlarged spleen ____________
19. Urinary retention ____________
20. Coma ____________
21. Halitosis ____________
22. Coin lesion, left lung ____________
23. All worn out ____________
24. Abnormal liver scan ____________
25. Dropsy ____________

Name ________________________

Injury and Poisoning - I (800-999)

2008 ICD-9-CM

This unit contains the diagnoses for fractures, dislocations, sprains, wounds, contusions, burns, poisonings, and other toxic effects and complications. Poisonings are easy to find using the Table of Drugs and Chemicals at the end of the Alphabetic Index.

Caution: Watch out (again) for the codes requiring a fifth digit. Also, what kind of injury would result from the incident in item 12 on the next page? Search on that term.

Using the Tabular List only, identify the three-digit category for:

1. Penicillin poisoning ____________
2. Anaphylactic shock ____________
3. Wrist sprain ____________
4. Frostbite ____________
5. Fracture temporal bone ____________
6. Open wound of toe ____________
7. Mechanical complication of dialysis shunt ____________
8. Burn of fingers ____________
9. Elbow dislocation ____________
10. Infected blister ____________

Name ______________________

Injury and Poisoning - II (800-999)

Using the alphabetic and/or tabular references, locate the following diseases and code to acceptable specificity, three, four, or five characters.

1. Air embolus following transfusion ____________
2. C5-C7 cord injury with complete lesion ____________
3. Open wound of scalp ____________
4. Concussion, still in coma after 48 hours ____________
5. Open dislocation, acromioclavicular joint ____________
6. Sunstroke ____________
7. Battered spouse syndrome ____________
8. Laceration and chemical burn, lower arm ____________
9. Lead oxide paint poisoning ____________
10. Peritonitis due to retained surgical sponge ____________
11. Third degree burn, upper back ____________
12. Dropped heavy trunk on left great toe ____________
13. Fifteen infected mosquito bites ____________
14. Struck by lightning while golfing ____________
15. Open fracture of metatarsal bones ____________
16. Rejection of kidney transplant ____________
17. Leaking silicone breast implant ____________
18. Abrasion, left leg ____________
19. Starvation ____________
20. Death by drowning ____________
21. Open fracture of the sternum ____________
22. Esophageal burns, drank "Easy-Off" oven cleaner ____________
23. Sprained ankle ____________
24. Pneumothorax from stab wound to chest ____________
25. Removed 3 small stones from left ear canal ____________

Name ______________________

Supplementary Classification - "V" Codes - I (V01-V86)

2008 ICD-9-CM

These codes are used as a "diagnosis" for a person who: (a) is receiving services for a specific purpose but is not currently sick, such as vaccination; (b) seeks treatment for a specific disorder such as chemotherapy; or (c) has some circumstance or problem present that influences the patient's health status but is not itself a current illness or injury, such as a history of cancer. Insurers may not pay for some of these codes, as they may question the medical necessity of treatment for well persons. Many managed care plans providing preventive care expect the office to use these codes when the patient is seen for routine care.

Caution: Some terms are not easy to find in the Alphabetic Index.

Using the Tabular List only, identify the V and two-digit category for:

1. Infant screened for chromosomal anomalies ____________
2. Artificial eye fitting ____________
3. Family planning ____________
4. Measles screening ____________
5. Triplets ____________
6. Seen for ear piercing ____________
7. MMR immunization ____________
8. Mother died of breast CA ____________
9. Exposure to hepatitis ____________
10. Patient "worried well" ____________

Name ________________________

Supplementary Classification - "V" Codes - II (V01-V86)

Using the alphabetic and/or tabular references, locate the following diseases and code to acceptable specificity, three, four, or five characters.

1. Counseling, contraceptive foam use ____________
2. Camp physical exam ____________
3. Twin delivery, 1 stillborn ____________
4. Male, family history of breast CA ____________
5. Adult, was battered as a child ____________
6. Drug allergy by history ____________
7. Cornea donor ____________
8. Going to India, needs cholera vaccine ____________
9. Check status of cystostomy ____________
10. Spent night with syphilitic partner ____________
11. Refugee exam ____________
12. Viral hepatitis carrier ____________
13. Drunk driving test ____________
14. Treated for alcoholism, 1986 ____________
15. Routine chest x-ray, food handler ____________
16. Problems with mother-in-law ____________
17. Orthodontia patient ____________
18. Receiving estrogen, postmenopausal ____________
19. Annual Pap smear exam ____________
20. Respirator dependent ____________
21. Recently in India, worried about exposure to cholera ____________
22. Allergy testing ____________
23. Diabetic lifestyle education ____________
24. Screening for sickle-cell disorder ____________
25. C-section delivery of stillborn sextuplets ____________

Name ____________________

Supplementary Classification - "E" Codes - I (E800-E999)

2008 ICD-9-CM

These codes describe the external causes of injury or poisoning. They would be used in addition to the actual condition treated. If you set a fractured femur caused by an automobile accident, code the fracture first (primary) and the E code second. The use of the E code could indicate that the primary responsibility for payment rests with some other agency beside the health insurance carrier, such as a taxicab company or the railroad.

Caution: Read the instructions carefully before beginning the coding exercises. Note that the reference to the fourth digit results in a five-character code.

Using the Tabular List only, identify the E and three-digit category for:

1. Train collided with downed tree E801.9 ✓
2. Wood alcohol poisoning E860.2 ✓
3. Fell from ski-lift gondola E847 ✓
4. Cigarette burn E898.1 ✓
5. Accidental aspirin poisoning E850.3 ✓
6. Fell out of bed E884.4 ✓
7. Injured by letter bomb E965.7 ✓
8. Accidentally pushed from moving car E818.9 ✓
9. Trampled by crowd in a panic E917.1
10. Radiation therapy overdose E873.2

Name Jenn Mead

Supplementary Classification - "E" Codes - II (E800-E999)

Using the alphabetic and/or tabular references, locate the following diseases and code to acceptable specificity, three, four, or five characters.

1. Sea anemone sting E905.6
2. Passenger hurt when snowmobile hit tree E820
3. Killed by handgun, possible homicide ______
4. Bicyclist injured by train ______
5. Bicyclist collided with wall ______
6. Slashed wrists in suicide attempt ______
7. Loss of hearing from rock music ______
8. Injured during earthquake ______
9. Diving accident, hit bottom of pool ______
10. Hurt at camp site, motor home steps collapsed ______
11. Thrown from horse & buggy in collision with car ______
12. Injured when hot air balloon crashed ______
13. 4 y/o drank gasoline from pop bottle ______
14. Injured by fireworks ______
15. Overcome by Agent Orange in Vietnam ______
16. Failure of aortic valve prosthesis, 4 days post-op ______
17. Severe reaction, used prescribed dose of eye meds ______
18. Burned while tending fireplace at cottage ______
19. Dehydration, water to home turned off ______
20. Human bites, left arm, 3 y/o male ______
21. Drowned when washed overboard during storm ______
22. Infection, contaminated during heart cath ______
23. Hand slashed by circular saw ______
24. Accidental ether poisoning at fraternity party ______
25. Skin frozen, contact with dry ice ______

Name ______________________

PUTTING IT ALL TOGETHER

This series of case studies asks you to find the correct procedure and diagnosis codes. Note also that you are asked to include any required modifier. The answers and the rationale for the answer follow this section. Read the case studies carefully, look for key terms, and be certain to follow all coding rules from CPT and ICD-9-CM.

1. The patient had a moderately progressive keratoconus and no longer has adequate functional vision. To delay the need for corneal transplant, Dr. Light scheduled the patient for intrastromal corneal ring segmental implants.

   Proc/Mod ____________ Diagnosis ____________

   ____________ ____________

   ____________ ____________

   ____________ ____________

2. A 22-year-old male was admitted to a residential psychiatric facility for treatment of an exacerbation of Asperger's syndrome. Following a comprehensive workup, he had 25 minutes of biofeedback psychotherapy on the day of admission.

   Proc/Mod ____________ Diagnosis ____________

   ____________ ____________

   ____________ ____________

   ____________ ____________

3. In June, Dr. Walton spent 35 minutes supervising and coordinating the care of his patient, 83-year-old John Roberts. John left the nursing home and moved into assisted living at the Maple Senior Center where he will be under the care of Maple Home Services. Mr. Roberts had recovered sufficiently from his left-sided paralysis following a stroke, and, since he was right-handed, he could now feed and dress himself. Mr. Roberts had a mild monoplegia of the left lower leg so Dr. Walton provided him with a folding wheeled walker for ambulation.

   Proc/Mod ____________ Diagnosis ____________

   ____________ ____________

   ____________ ____________

   ____________ ____________

Name ________________________

4. Dr. Jack Armstrong, a rehabilitation specialist, discharged Mary Martin from City Hospital following surgery to repair a pathologic fracture of the right hip. The same day, the doctor admitted her to the Meadows Continuing Care facility for physical therapy and long term care.

Proc/Mod	____________	Diagnosis	____________
	____________		____________
	____________		____________
	____________		____________

5. Michael Jaydan injured his left thumb playing basketball. He was seen in Dr. Spaulding's after hours urgent care center. The doctor performed a new patient EPF visit and took two x-rays of the thumb. There was no fracture. Dr. Spaulding treated the sprain injury by strapping the thumb with a 3-inch elastic compression bandage.

Proc/Mod	____________	Diagnosis	____________
	____________		____________
	____________		____________
	____________		____________

6. Paul Brown was scheduled at Metropolitan Hospital for outpatient surgery to replace his mature right cataract with a lens implant. Just as Dr. Black was to begin the procedure, Mr. Brown developed a significant cardiac dysrhythmia. The surgery was cancelled and Dr. Black admitted Mr. Brown to the hospital's observation unit for care of the arrhythmia. Dr. Green, a cardiologist, later that day admitted Mr. Brown to Metropolitan Hospital for a complete cardiac workup.

   Report the services of Dr. Black.

Proc/Mod	____________	Diagnosis	____________
	____________		____________
	____________		____________
	____________		____________

7. An ambulance brought a 37-year-old man to the Central City Hospital ER after he was injured in a hit and run accident. The orthopedic surgeon, Dr. Frost, treated the patient in the emergency department for a fractured phalanx, right ring finger; a fractured mandible on the right; and the closed treatment of a fractured right femur. When the patient was stable, Dr. Robins admitted him to Central City Hospital for continuing care of the fractures. Code Dr. Frost's services.

Proc/Mod	____________	Diagnosis	____________
	____________		____________
	____________		____________
	____________		____________

Name ________________________

8. Dr. Dallas discharged 79-year-old Mary Stuart from Mercy Medical Center after she recovered from an extrinsic status asthmaticus attack. She was seen that afternoon in his office for wheezing that did not respond to an albuterol nebulizer treatment. She was readmitted to Mercy for further care.

Proc/Mod	____________	Diagnosis	____________
	____________		____________
	____________		____________
	____________		____________

9. Jennifer Taylor, age 4, was seen by her osteopathic pediatrician after she had been ill for two days with a productive cough and now had developed a fever. Her examination focused on the presenting problems. The doctor diagnosed bronchitis and a somatic dysfunction of the cervical, thoracic, rib, and abdominal areas. She was treated with medication and OMT.

Proc/Mod	____________	Diagnosis	____________
	____________		____________
	____________		____________
	____________		____________

10. Harry Morgan, who has Type II diabetes and severe osteoarthritis, was seen to discuss his recent lab work. When he appeared uncoordinated and confused, Dr. Jessup did a glucose test with a reagent strip that showed his glucose level was low. Mr. Morgan was given crackers and a drink and later retested. Dr. Jessup became concerned that Harry was not taking his medications correctly or perhaps had developed a new problem, so he ordered a comprehensive metabolic panel. Mr. Morgan was in the office for over an hour and monitored closely by the doctor.

Proc/Mod	____________	Diagnosis	____________
	____________		____________
	____________		____________
	____________		____________

Name ________________________

11. When Dr. Davis saw Ralph Cramer in a subsequent inpatient visit today, the patient stated he wanted to get out of the hospital in time for his granddaughter's birthday party tomorrow. His only complaints were some back pain from spending a week in a hospital bed. The doctor ordered a final lab test to confirm that the severe urinary tract infection that required the hospitalization was no longer present. Dr. Davis told Mr. Cramer he would return by noon tomorrow and, if the lab work showed no problems, he would send him home at that time.

Proc/Mod ____________ Diagnosis ____________

____________ ____________

____________ ____________

____________ ____________

12. Fred Smith returned to his cardiologist's office for a six-month recheck of the medications for his hypertensive heart disease. His EKG showed abnormalities, so Dr. Peck ordered a cardiovascular stress test to be done before Mr. Smith left the office. The doctor's physician assistant supervised the test and prepared the tracing for Dr. Peck's interpretation. The stress test revealed ischemia, possibly related to a recent "silent" myocardial infarction. Mr. Smith was scheduled for further workup.

Proc/Mod ____________ Diagnosis ____________

____________ ____________

____________ ____________

____________ ____________

13. The patient was seen in his family doctor's office as an emergency. He was treated with an insect venom injection for anaphylaxis, secondary to a bee sting.

Proc/Mod ____________ Diagnosis ____________

____________ ____________

____________ ____________

____________ ____________

Name ______________________

14. A 19-year-old male took his girlfriend hunting. Her shotgun accidentally discharged in the duck blind and he was hit just below the right eye by ricocheted shot. He had no change in vision but did have a small laceration and bruising in the area. Films in the emergency department revealed a metal foreign body embedded in the eyelid, just below the laceration. The laceration was sutured and the foreign body removed by the ER physician. The patient was advised to see his primary care physician for follow-up care. The gunshot accident was reported to the authorities. The foreign body was given to the patient, who wanted it as a "souvenir."

Proc/Mod ____________ Diagnosis ____________

____________ ____________

____________ ____________

____________ ____________

15. A new patient was seen in the office for trauma to the left elbow received in a fall. Two x-rays of the elbow revealed no fracture. The patient was advised to rest the arm and use hot or cold compresses on the swelling, depending on which made it feel better. He was asked to contact the office if it wasn't better in 5-7 days. As the patient was about to leave the exam room, he asked the doctor to remove the cerumen from both ears. This was done with a curette and lavage.

Proc/Mod ____________ Diagnosis ____________

____________ ____________

____________ ____________

____________ ____________

16. Dr. Brady, a pediatrician in solo practice, performed a routine newborn exam on Baby Boy Peterson. Later that day the baby developed a severe, but not critical, respiratory distress and was transferred to the care of Dr. Lewis, a neonatologist, who admitted the baby to the neonatal intensive care unit (NICU).

Dr. Brady's
Proc/Mod ____________ Diagnosis ____________

____________ ____________

Dr. Lewis's
Proc/Mod ____________ Diagnosis ____________

____________ ____________

Name ______________________

17. The client was seen in a full session psychotherapy visit for a posttraumatic stress disorder. Dr. Bauer asked her to stay longer for biofeedback training to help her stop smoking and reduce stress.

Proc/Mod ____________ Diagnosis ____________

____________ ____________

____________ ____________

____________ ____________

18. Dr. Franklin left a group practice in East Jordan and set up private practice in Summerville, a town about twenty-five miles west of East Jordan. Some of her patients followed her to the new practice. She set up new records for these patients and incorporated copies of the group practice records in these charts. She saw Robert Taylor (an expanded problem focused visit) for the six-month renewal of his prescriptions for Type II diabetes.

Proc/Mod ____________ Diagnosis ____________

____________ ____________

____________ ____________

____________ ____________

19. The 13-year-old patient had an abscess on the right middle finger and a cyst of the left first toe. Both lesions were treated at the same operative session.

Proc/Mod ____________ Diagnosis ____________

____________ ____________

____________ ____________

____________ ____________

20. John Williams, a 59-year-old real estate agent, complained of occasional rectal bleeding over the past year. He was scheduled for a diagnostic flexible sigmoidoscopy. The surgeon also removed three polyps using bipolar cautery. Two polyps were removed intact while the third polyp had to be removed piecemeal. All lesions were proximal to the splenic flexure.

Proc/Mod ____________ Diagnosis ____________

____________ ____________

____________ ____________

____________ ____________

Name ________________________

21. Frank Johnson had worsening pain in his right knee over the past year. Dr. Butler performed a diagnostic arthroscopy that included a partial medial menisectomy and chondroplasty of two compartments of the knee.

Proc/Mod ____________ Diagnosis ____________

____________ ____________

____________ ____________

____________ ____________

22. The emergency room doctor at City Hospital diagnosed a 20-week missed abortion for Martha Thomas. She was treated with prostaglandin and subsequently delivered all the products of conception.

Proc/Mod ____________ Diagnosis ____________

____________ ____________

____________ ____________

____________ ____________

23. George Smith had not seen Dr. Mann for two years when he returned to the office concerned about some "red bumps" on his face, neck, and arms. After an EPF visit to Dr. Mann who diagnosed the "bumps" as actinic keratoses, the doctor removed a skin tag from the neck/shoulder area where it had been irritated by Mr. Smith's shirt collars.

Proc/Mod ____________ Diagnosis ____________

____________ ____________

____________ ____________

____________ ____________

24. Phyllis Young had been hospitalized for a day when her doctor asked Dr. Samuel Sterns, a surgeon, to see her for abdominal pain. Dr. Sterns examined her and diagnosed gallstones. He scheduled Ms. Young for a laparoscopic cholecystectomy later that day.

Proc/Mod ____________ Diagnosis ____________

____________ ____________

____________ ____________

____________ ____________

Name ______________________

25. A mother brought her 6-month-old infant to the office for a flu immunization and was seen by the nurse. The nurse reviewed the vaccine information sheet with the mother and gave her a copy of the document. The mother stated that she noticed that her son had a cough but there had been no change in his behavior and he did not act as though he were ill. He had no fever. The nurse checked and documented the child's vital signs, and noted that there were no contraindications to administering the vaccine at today's visit.

Proc/Mod ____________ Diagnosis ____________

____________ ____________

____________ ____________

____________ ____________

Putting It All Together—Answers and Rationales

1. Proc/Mod: 0099T Diagnosis: 371.60

   The procedure is new and appears in CPT as a Category III Code. Keratoconus is listed as either stable (a slow, persistent worsening) or acute (sudden, severe onset). Since neither describes a moderately progressive disease state, code the diagnosis as unspecified.

2. Proc/Mod: 99305, 90875 Diagnosis: 299.80

   CPT states that medical psychotherapy is reported in addition to the E/M service.

3. Proc/Mod: 99316, E0143 Diagnosis: 438.22, 438.42

   There was medical treatment at the nursing facility and the time exceeded 30 minutes. The service would be a discharge of more than 30 minutes from a nursing facility rather than the care plan oversight service. Providing the walker is code E0143. The diagnoses must relate to late effects of a stroke (438.xx), not on the acute event. Note how the late effect of cerebrovascular disease (438) is focused on the sequelae following the causal event.

4. Proc/Mod: 99238, 99305 Diagnosis: 733.14

   Because two facilities are involved, the discharge from the acute care hospital and the admission to the nursing facility may both be reported. Since the patient's condition is familiar to the doctor, it us unlikely that the discharge would exceed 30 minutes and the nursing facility admission reflects the moderate severity of the patient's condition. Caution: some payers may not allow the same physician to report two medical services on the same day.

5. Proc/Mod: 99202-25, 73120-LT, 29280-FA, A6448 Diagnosis: 842.10

   The modifier –25 would allow payment of the office visit when a treatment is performed at the same visit. When reporting strapping, remember to include the required supplies. A fracture was not confirmed. Note that "sprain, thumb" refers to 842.10, a sprain of "unspecified site" of the hand even though the site was identified.

6. Proc/Mod: 99235 Diagnosis: 366.17, 427.9

   Procedure code 99235, rather than 99219, is correct because Dr. Black admitted and discharged (by a transfer of care) Mr. Brown on the same day. Dr. Green will report the initial hospital care service, 99221-99223. The diagnosis codes would be the cataract first and arrhythmia second. "When a patient presents for outpatient surgery and develops complications requiring admission to observation, code the reason for the surgery as the first reported diagnosis (reason for the encounter), followed by codes for the complications as secondary diagnoses." (Guidelines, A 2)

7. Proc/Mod: 27500, 21450-51, 26600-51-F8 Diagnosis: 821.00, 802.20, 816.00

Remember to put the most significant surgery on the first line, regardless of how they are listed on the operative note. Since the descriptions did not refer to a manipulation, use codes that state "no manipulation." Modifier –51 or –59 is required on the 2nd and 3rd services, as well as the modifier describing the finger. Diagnosis codes will be "unspecified" since the site or part was not identified.

8. Proc/Mod: 99238, 94640, J7613, 99221-25 Diagnosis: 493.01, 786.07, 493.92

This is an example of claims you will need to monitor. There are three claims: one for each hospitalization and one for the office services. The office visit is not billed, as those services are related to the hospital admission of the same day. Modifier –25 is required for the admission, as it is not related to the other E/M service (discharge) reported that day. The diagnosis for the discharge service, 493.01, describes the findings of her hospital stay. The diagnosis for the office services would be the symptom, wheezing, 786.07; the admission diagnosis: 493.92, Asthma, with acute exacerbation. Be prepared to fight for payment on this one.

9. Proc/Mod: 99212-25, 98926 Diagnosis: 490, 739.9

Use modifier –25 on the office visit to indicate that the diagnosis was made today. Do not count on the fact there are two diagnoses to explain that the services are not related. Note the body regions identified in CPT for the CPT OMT codes. The diagnosis 490, bronchitis, is not specified as acute or chronic. The somatic dysfunction codes would be 739.1, 739.2, 739.8, and 739.9. Since 739.9 states abdomen and others, it is the diagnosis code for the OMT service.

10. Proc/Mod: 99215, 82948, 82948-91 Diagnosis: 250.00

The extended office visit is based on time, not the level of the examination. The repeat lab test needs the –91 modifier. The metabolic panel was ordered, not performed in the office. The severe osteoarthritis did not impact today's visit so that diagnosis is not reported.

11. Proc/Mod: 99231 Diagnosis: 784.5. 599.0

A higher level of inpatient visit would be incorrect. The patient must be stable if he is to be discharged tomorrow. Today's complaint, back pain, would be the diagnosis for this visit and the urinary tract infection would be reported as the diagnosis for the lab work ordered.

12. Proc/Mod: 99213, 93000-59, 93015 Diagnosis: 402.90, 794.31

The office visit is likely to be an expanded problem focused visit. The 12-lead EKG would require the –59 modifier or payers might bundle it in with the stress test. The diagnosis 402.90 would be used for the office visit and the EKG, while the best diagnosis for the stress test is the abnormal EKG code, 794.31. Avoid the diagnosis "ischemia," as the cause has not been determined and cannot be labeled chronic based on this information.

13. Proc/Mod: 99215-25, 95130 Diagnosis: 995.0, 989.5, E905.3

This is a problem of high severity. Modifier –25 should be used to indicate the office visit was separate from the injection. Use 995.0 for the office visit, and 989.5 (toxic effect of venom) for the injection. Reporting E905.3 may be optional.

14. Proc/Mod: 67938-54, 12011-54-51 Diagnosis: 930.8, 870.0, E922.1

Since the removal of an embedded foreign body is the major procedure, it should be reported first. Use modifier –54 on both procedures to indicate the services are surgical care only. The services relate to only one area of the body so there probably would be no E/M service. Use diagnosis code 930.8 rather than 930.9, as the site is specified, but not as conjunctival sac (930.1) or the lacimal punctum (930.2). If the documentation supported an E/M service, such as abrasions from other pieces of shot, it would be 99281-25, indicating it is unrelated to the surgical service. The gunshot accident code, E922.1, may be optional.

15. Proc/Mod: 99201-25, 73070-LT, 69210 Diagnosis: 923.11, 380.4

The examination was focused on the elbow and requires –25, separate from the surgical service, 69210. Use modifier –LT on the x-ray. Get into the habit of using right and left indicators even though they are not required. Since there was no fracture or open wound, the diagnosis must be contusion for the first two services. Use impacted cerumen, 380.4, for the 69210.

16. Dr. Brady's Proc/Mod: 99431 Diagnosis: V20.2

Dr. Lewis's Proc/Mod: 99223 Diagnosis: 770.89

Dr. Brady's service was the newborn exam and is billable since he is not in practice with the neonatologist. The diagnosis, at the time of his visit, would have been a normal newborn. The problem occurred later. This was not stated as a "critical" admission, so the regular initial care services would be reported, but it would be reasonable to report a high level of service.

17. Proc/Mod: 90806, 90901-51 Diagnosis: 309.81, 305.11

Use the two codes rather than 90876, which combines the two services into one code. Modifier –51 or –59 clarifies two separate services. The diagnosis could be reported as PTSD (309.81) for both services, or PTSD and tobacco abuse (305.11) for the biofeedback. Avoid using codes from psychological trauma (V15.41, V15.42) or psychosocial circumstances (V62.89). For mental health services, it is advisable to code on the "light" side. Reveal no more than necessary to get the claim paid.

18. Proc/Mod: 99213 Diagnosis: 250.00

Assuming that she was the doctor who prescribed the meds six months ago, this would be an established patient visit. If Mr. Taylor is transferring to her practice and has had no professional services in the past three years from Dr. Franklin or another physician of the same specialty in her former practice, this would be a new patient visit, 99202. The change in tax identification numbers and establishing a new chart does not make this a new patient visit.

19. Proc/Mod: 10061 Diagnosis: 681.00, 706.2

Do not report two codes, 10060-F7 and 10060-TA, as the description for 10061 states "multiple." Code 10061 would be the correct procedure code even though the treatment areas are separate. Report both diagnoses; the order of the diagnosis codes would not matter.

20. Proc/Mod: 45384 Diagnosis: 211.3

CPT states, "surgical endoscopy always includes diagnostic endoscopy." Code 45384 is used once, regardless of the number of polyps removed. Also, it makes no difference if the polyp is removed whole or in pieces. The diagnosis should be polyp of the colon, rather than rectal bleeding. As there is no mention of malignancy, be certain you select a code from the benign section.

21. Proc/Mod: 29881-RT, 29877-51-RT, G0287-51-RT Diagnosis: 717.82, 717.7

The arthroscopic menisectomy is the major procedure and should be reported first. Chondroplasty is reported only once no matter how many areas of the knee are debrided. However, CMS created a code, G0289, for reporting chondroplasty on a separate compartment.Modifier –51 or –59 would be reported first as it is a pricing modifier; modifier –RT explains that only the right knee was involved in the surgery. If you work for an orthopedic surgeon, contact the payers to determine if they will accept the G-code and if they allow it to be reported with a quantity of more than 1. A torn meniscus could be a current or an old injury. Report the old injury (717.82) for the first service, and chondromalacia (717.7) for the other two services.

22. Proc/Mod: 59855 Diagnosis: 632

Note that the procedure code includes all the visits associated with the abortion service. The diagnosis is one of the few three-digit codes in the section on pregnancy and childbirth.

23. Proc/Mod: 99213-25, 11200 Diagnosis: 702.0, 701.9

The visit is reported separately, as the visit was more complex than the usual preoperative evaluation and postoperative care for a single skin tag. Modifier –25 is required for the office visit. Do not report –59 on the surgery and omit the –25 on the visit, as the 99213 was when the irritated skin tag was found.

24. Proc/Mod: 99252-57, 47562 Diagnosis: 789.00, 574.20

Dr. Sterns's first visit with the patient was the consultation, and the –57 indicates that the decision to do surgery was made then. However, a directive from Medicare in January 2006 states this would be a "transfer of care" since her primary care doctor no longer plans to treat her for this abdominal pain. CMS states this is not a consultation but would be reported as an initial or subsequent visit. Since the admitting physician (the primary care doctor) reports the initial day of inpatient care, Dr. Sterns would report a subsequent hospital visit, 99231 or 99232, with the modifier –57. If this Medicare rule becomes part of a future CPT, this rule would apply to all payers.

25. Proc/Mod: 99211-25, 90657, 90471 Diagnosis: V04.81

This is a good example of the proper use of code 99211. Had the child been examined yesterday and returned today for the immunization, you would report only the immunization (90657) and the administration service (90471).

EXAM QUESTIONS FOR CPT, CPT AND HCPCS, AND ICD-9-CM

Directions:

- Use the appropriate coding manual to determine the correct choice for each situation.
- Answer sheet is provided at the end of each exam for recording your choice for each question.

Name ________________________

Exam Questions for CPT

Directions: Use the appropriate coding manual to determine the correct choice for each situation.

1. Patient underwent nerve grafting of the right foot, 3 cm.

   ① 64885

   ② 64890

   ③ 64891

   ④ 64901

2. Patient underwent thyroidectomy for removal of remaining thyroid tissue after previous right lobectomy for suspected malignancy.

   ① 60225

   ② 60240

   ③ 60260

   ④ 60270

3. Established nursing facility resident was seen for annual assessment.

   ① 99201

   ② 99310

   ③ 99318

   ④ 99336

4. An 81-year-old patient receives anesthesia prior to undergoing cardioversion for persistent arrhythmia. Include physical status modifier with code.

   ① 00400-P2 + 99100

   ② 00410-P2

   ③ 00410-P2 + 99100

   ④ 00410-P4

5. Surgeon performs a sphenoid sinusotomy for removal of polyps, including biopsy.

   ① 31020

   ② 31050

   ③ 31051

   ④ 31070

6. Physician performs a surgical biopsy of the right temporal artery.

   ① 37200

   ② 37605

   ③ 37609

   ④ 37799

7. A 67-year-old patient underwent contact laser vaporization of the prostate.

   ① 52450

   ② 52601

   ③ 52647

   ④ 52648

8. Patient underwent total abdominal hysterectomy, sparing the tubes and ovaries.

   ① 58150

   ② 58152

   ③ 58200

   ④ 58210

9. Radiologist directs and interprets the placement of a long gastrostomy tube in a patient who is status post cerebrovascular accident.

   ① 43246-26

   ② 74340

   ③ 74355

   ④ 74363

10. Nursing home patient was admitted for management of pneumonia which is now resolved. The physician came by the facility to discharge the patient to home, spending 20 minutes with the patient and family.

    ① 99217

    ② 99238

    ③ 99315

    ④ 99339

11. The physician conducted an initial office consultation for a 44-year-old patient, 6 years status post lumbar laminectomy, with intractable sciatic pain, depression, and history of narcotic dependency/abuse, high complexity.

① 99241

② 99243

③ 99244

④ 99245

12. A 16-year-old patient undergoes excision of an aneurysmal bone cyst of the proximal right humerus, with allograft.

① 23155

② 23156

③ 23184

④ 23220

13. A 15-year-old, otherwise healthy patient receives anesthesia for electroconvulsive therapy. Include physical status modifier with code.

① 00104-P1

② 00104-P2

③ 00190-P1

④ 00210-P1

14. Patient who is status post cochlear implant has visit for group rehabilitation, treatment of speech, and a processing disorder.

① 92506

② 92508

③ 92520

④ 92557

15. Healthcare employee receives first of three Hepatitis B vaccination, intramuscular injection.

① 90371 + 90772

② 90746

③ 90746 + 90772

④ 90740 + 90471

16. Patient underwent cervical conization with loop electrical excision of the transitional zone.

① 57460

② 57500

③ 57520

④ 57522

17. Patient underwent stereotactic biopsy of intracranial lesion under MR guidance.

① 61720

② 61750

③ 61751

④ 61770

18. Dr. Harris counsels a group of teenagers regarding sexually transmitted diseases and prevention. Session lasts 30 minutes.

① 99401

② 99402

③ 99411

④ 99411-21

19. Dr. Nuri examines an 18-year-old in the emergency department for recurrent, severe menstrual migraine headache.

① 99241

② 99281

③ 99282

④ 99284

20. Patient underwent in-office simple incision and drainage of a pilonidal cyst.

① 10060

② 10061

③ 10080

④ 10081

21. Surgeon removes a Harrington rod in a patient with chronic irritation in the region of insertion.

① 22849

② 22850

③ 22852

④ 22899

22. Patient with congenital cleft palate underwent rhinoplasty with columellar lengthening, including the septum and tip.

① 30410

② 30430

③ 30460

④ 30462

23. Patient with suspected apnea underwent sleep study with recording of ventilation, respiratory effort, heart rate, and oxygen saturation. Technologist was in attendance.

① 95805

② 95806

③ 95807

④ 95811

24. Surgeon performed excision of pterygium with grafting, left eye.

① 65400

② 65420-LT

③ 65426-LT

④ 67800

25. The neonatologist was asked to be on standby for 35 minutes for cesarean delivery of baby in distress.

① 99360

② 99360-22

③ 99436

④ 99440

26. Physician performed complex repair of a 3.2 cm. scalp laceration.

① 13120

② 13120 + 13122

③ 13121

④ 13121 + 13122

27. A 65-year-old patient receives anesthesia for repair of inguinal hernia. The patient has controlled hypertension. Include physical status modifier with code.

① 00830-P1

② 00830-P2

③ 00832-P1

④ 00832-P2

28. The patient underwent creation of burr holes of the skull with evacuation of subdural hematoma.

① 61105

② 61140

③ 61154

④ 61156

29. Five-year-old patient, status post eardrum rupture, undergoes tympanic membrane repair with patch.

① 69433

② 69610

③ 69620

④ 69631

30. David was scheduled to see Dr. Bronson for his six-month checkup and to have lab work done two weeks before his appointment on the 15th. As directed, the lab work was done on the first of the month. David called Dr. Bronson's office on the 3rd and talked to Dr. Bronson for 15 minutes about the tests. The doctor ordered two more tests done by the 5th so that the findings would be in the office for David's appointment on the 15th. What code would be reported for the service on the 3rd of the month?

① 99441

② 99442

③ 99443

④ 99444

31. Anesthesia was administered to patient for gastric bypass procedure performed due to patient's morbid obesity. Include physical status modifier with code.

① 00700-P3

② 00790-P2

③ 00790-P3

④ 00797-P3

32. Physician performed excision of inguinal hidradenitis with complex repair.

① 11450

② 11451

③ 11462

④ 11463

33. Patient was scheduled to undergo extensive internal and external hemorrhoidectomy with fistulectomy. Ten minutes prior to the start of the procedure, after anesthesia had been administered, the patient experienced a rapid decrease in heart rate and the physician canceled the procedure.

① 46260

② 46260-52

③ 46260-53

④ 46262-53

34. Patient underwent cystourethroscopy and laser ablation of two bladder tumors, each approximately 2.7 cm. in size.

① 52204

② 52214

③ 52234

④ 52235

35. Patient underwent excision of Peyronie plaque, 4.0 cm., with graft.

① 54060

② 54065

③ 54110

④ 54111

36. Hand specialist performs neuroplasty of the ulnar nerve of the left wrist.

① 64704-LT

② 64718-LT

③ 64719-LT

④ 64721-LT

37. Patient, age 15, is seen by his new doctor for a comprehensive physical examination and immunizations. Patient also has moderate acne on face and chest.

① 99394

② 99394-25

③ 99384

④ 99384-25

38. Patient underwent replantation of thumb after complete amputation from the distal tip to the MP joint.

① 20816

② 20822

③ 20824

④ 20827

39. Patient underwent operative laryngoscopy for removal of chicken bone fragment.

① 31511

② 31525

③ 31530

④ 31531

40. Patient with history of hypertriglyceridemia but with normal cholesterol levels has triglyceride level determined.

① 82465

② 83718

③ 84478

④ 84485

41. Asthma patient receives initial evaluation and first IPPB treatment.

① 94640

② 94645

③ 94660

④ 94664

42. Dr. Ladwig performs an independent medical examination for patient Mr. Smith to determine Worker's Compensation impairment rating.

① 99450

② 99455

③ 99456

④ 99499

43. Patient receives anesthesia for extracorporeal shock wave lithotripsy with water bath. Patient has mild asthma. Include physical status modifier with code.

① 00872-P1

② 00872-P2

③ 00873-P1

④ 00873-P2

44. Patient underwent single-lung transplant with cardiopulmonary bypass employed during the procedure.

① 32851

② 32852

③ 32853

④ 32854

45. Patient with intestinal intussusception undergoes reduction through laparotomy approach.

① 44005

② 44020

③ 44050

④ 44055

46. Surgeon performs gastric bypass procedure for the patient's morbid obesity with small intestine reconstruction to limit absorption.

① 43842

② 43846

③ 43847

④ 43848

47. Ms. Jones was seen in an initial office orthopedic consultation for bilateral trochanteric bursitis; visit was considered problem-focused only.

① 99201

② 99241

③ 99242

④ 99251

48. Surgeon performs repair of abdominal aortic aneurysm, caused by high-grade atherosclerosis.

① 35001

② 35081

③ 35082

④ 35091

49. Dr. Kelly successfully performs resuscitation for an infant suffering cardiac distress during delivery.

① 99432

② 99435

③ 99436

④ 99440

50. Patient underwent excision of 1.5 cm. malignant skin lesion of the left calf, as well as removal of Norplant contraceptive capsules.

① 11602 + 11976

② 11602 + 11976-51

③ 11976 + 11602

④ 11976 + 11602-51

51. Patient was seen in the office for trigger point injection involving the trapezius and latissimus muscle groups.

① 20551

② 20552

③ 64415

④ 64416

52. Patient underwent hepatic artery ligation with complex suture repair of a liver laceration following motor vehicle accident.

① 47350

② 47360

③ 47360-51

④ 47361

53. Hospital follow-up visit by Dr. Stephens to see a 59-year-old female patient, status post uncomplicated left hip fixation.

① 99221

② 99223

③ 99231

④ 99232

54. Family practitioner performed excision of a lipoma of the right forearm, 1.5 cm. in diameter.

① 11402

② 11402 + 12031

③ 11422

④ 11422 + 12031

55. Donor undergoes bone marrow harvesting for transplantation.

① 38220

② 38230

③ 38240

④ 38241

56. Patient underwent total gastrectomy with Roux-en-Y reconstruction for stomach carcinoma.

① 43620

② 43621

③ 43631

④ 43633

57. Surgeon performed a simple Burch urethropexy on 45-year-old, mentally underdeveloped female.

① 51800

② 51840

③ 51841

④ 51992

58. Newly diagnosed testicular cancer patient underwent radical orchiectomy with abdominal exploration via inguinal approach.

① 54520

② 54522

③ 54530

④ 54535

59. Patient had reconstruction of the mandibular rami due to blunt trauma, undergoing C osteotomy with bone graft.

① 21188

② 21193

③ 21194

④ 21195

60. Patient underwent bilateral cerebral carotid angiography under direct radiologic supervision.

① 75665

② 75671

③ 75676

④ 75680

61. The patient was seen on initial endocrinology office visit, having been referred for signs and symptoms of new-onset diabetes.

① 99201

② 99204

③ 99212

④ 99214

62. Patient underwent emergency laparoscopic appendectomy.

① 44950

② 44960

③ 44970

④ 44979

63. Patient underwent nephrolithotomy for removal of large staghorn calculus occupying the renal pelvis and calyces.

① 50010

② 50065

③ 50075

④ 50081

64. Patient underwent flexible sigmoidoscopy to 60 cm. with removal of two small polyps using snare technique.

① 45330

② 45333

③ 45338

④ 45385

65. Dr. Roberts conducts a home visit for a non-ambulatory patient with progressive multiple sclerosis, now experiencing respiratory difficulty. The physician spent a total of 45 minutes with the new patient and family discussing treatment options and possible admission to nursing facility.

① 99342

② 99343

③ 99348

④ 99349

66. Surgeon performed limited thoracotomy for lung biopsy.

① 32551

② 32035

③ 32095

④ 32100

67. Patient underwent marsupialization of Bartholin gland cyst.

① 10040

② 10060

③ 56420

④ 56440

68. Patient receives 15 minutes of ultrasound therapy to the left hip for bursitis.

① 97033

② 97035

③ 97110

④ 97124

69. Patient with symptoms of poisoning underwent testing for the presence of arsenic.

① 82157

② 82175

③ 83015

④ 83018

70. Patient underwent pericardial window creation for drainage of excess pericardial fluid.

① 33010

② 33015

③ 33020

④ 33025

71. Patient with simple papilloma of the penis undergoes cryosurgical removal.

① 54056

② 54057

③ 54065

④ 54110

72. Pain specialist physician performs single lumbar epidural steroid injection.

① 62280

② 62282

③ 62311

④ 62319

73. Patient underwent emergency noncontrast head CT scan following blunt trauma to the skull.

① 70450

② 70470

③ 70486

④ 70540

74. Nuclear medicine ventilation and perfusion lung scan was performed on a patient with sudden shortness of breath; aerosol technique was used, two projections were obtained.

① 78584

② 78587

③ 78588

④ 78594

75. Patient was treated with aortofemoral-popliteal venous bypass grafting for severe occlusive disease.

① 35456

② 35548

③ 35551

④ 35651

76. A 12-year-old female patient underwent dilation of the urethra under general anesthesia.

① 53605

② 53660

③ 53661

④ 53665

77. Patient underwent radial keratotomy procedure in the right eye.

① 65710-RT

② 65760-RT

③ 65767-RT

④ 65771-RT

78. Combative patient underwent removal of burrowed insect from external auditory canal; general anesthesia required.

① 69145

② 69200

③ 69205

④ 69220

79. Expectant mother of twins underwent complete obstetrical ultrasound in second trimester.

① 76805 + 76810

② 76811 + 76812

③ 76815

④ 76856

80. Patient Young, on parole, was to undergo his first monthly drug testing for marijuana. The lab ran a test to detect the patient's THC level. Two-phase procedure was performed.

① 80100

② 80100 + 80102

③ 80102 quantity 2

④ 80103

81. Steelworker seen in the emergency room for acute eye pain associated with probable steel shaving in the affected eye, now gone.

① 99281

② 99283

③ 99284

④ 99285

82. Surgeon performs closure of rectovaginal fistula by vaginal approach.

① 57284

② 57300

③ 57305

④ 57310

83. Patient underwent before and after contrast MRI studies of the pelvis.

① 72191

② 72193

③ 72197

④ 72198

84. Surgeon performed open repair of a femoral neck fracture with internal fixation.

① 27230

② 27235

③ 27236

④ 27244

85. Patient underwent tubal ligation with use of Falope rings, vaginal approach.

① 58600

② 58615

③ 58671

④ 58700

86. Patient receives chiropractic manipulative treatment for pain in the temporomandibular joint region.

① 97140

② 98925

③ 98940

④ 98943

87. Patient undergoes sex-change operation, from male to female.

① 55899

② 55970

③ 55980

④ 58999

88. Surgeon performed cesarean delivery after failed VBAC attempt.

① 59514

② 59610

③ 59612

④ 59620

89. Patient underwent cataract extraction with insertion of intraocular lens via phacoemulsification technique.

① 66830

② 66850

③ 66982

④ 66984

90. The CPT Category III codes are updated quarterly.

① True

② False

91. The doctor orders a urinalysis to screen for bacteria.

① 81000

② 81002

③ 81003

④ 81007

92. The patient has an automated CBC, WBC, and platelet count.

① 85025

② 85027

③ 85041

④ 85048

93. Dr. Roberts orders a test for total Hepatitis A antibodies.

① 86706

② 86707

③ 86708

④ 86709

94. The patient underwent debridement and dressing of a small burn of the forearm in Dr. Gray's office.

① 16000

② 16020

③ 16025

④ 16030

95. The patient underwent pelvic magnetic resonance imaging before and after contrast to rule out a pelvic mass.

① 72194

② 72195

③ 72196

④ 72197

96. Mary Johnson had a closed manipulation of her distal fibular fracture.

① 27780

② 27786

③ 27788

④ 27792

97. The radiologist supervises and interprets lymphangiography of both upper arms.

① 75801-26

② 75803-26

③ 75805-26

④ 75807-26

98. Patient is hospitalized for a mobilization rearrangement repair of a conjunctival laceration.

① 65270

② 65272

③ 65273

④ 65285

99. The operative note states the patient underwent excision of a lesion of the mucosa and underlying muscle of the vestibule of the mouth.

① 40812

② 40814

③ 40816

④ 40820

100. Dr. Jones performed a C1-C2 anterior arthrodesis.

① 22548

② 22554 + 22585

③ 22595

④ 22600 + 22614

Name ________________________

Answers to Exam Questions: CPT

1. ① ② ③ ④
2. ① ② ③ ④
3. ① ② ③ ④
4. ① ② ③ ④
5. ① ② ③ ④
6. ① ② ③ ④
7. ① ② ③ ④
8. ① ② ③ ④
9. ① ② ③ ④
10. ① ② ③ ④
11. ① ② ③ ④
12. ① ② ③ ④
13. ① ② ③ ④
14. ① ② ③ ④
15. ① ② ③ ④
16. ① ② ③ ④
17. ① ② ③ ④
18. ① ② ③ ④
19. ① ② ③ ④
20. ① ② ③ ④
21. ① ② ③ ④
22. ① ② ③ ④
23. ① ② ③ ④
24. ① ② ③ ④
25. ① ② ③ ④
26. ① ② ③ ④
27. ① ② ③ ④
28. ① ② ③ ④
29. ① ② ③ ④
30. ① ② ③ ④
31. ① ② ③ ④
32. ① ② ③ ④
33. ① ② ③ ④
34. ① ② ③ ④
35. ① ② ③ ④
36. ① ② ③ ④
37. ① ② ③ ④
38. ① ② ③ ④
39. ① ② ③ ④
40. ① ② ③ ④
41. ① ② ③ ④
42. ① ② ③ ④
43. ① ② ③ ④
44. ① ② ③ ④
45. ① ② ③ ④
46. ① ② ③ ④
47. ① ② ③ ④
48. ① ② ③ ④
49. ① ② ③ ④
50. ① ② ③ ④
51. ① ② ③ ④
52. ① ② ③ ④
53. ① ② ③ ④
54. ① ② ③ ④
55. ① ② ③ ④
56. ① ② ③ ④
57. ① ② ③ ④
58. ① ② ③ ④
59. ① ② ③ ④
60. ① ② ③ ④
61. ① ② ③ ④
62. ① ② ③ ④
63. ① ② ③ ④
64. ① ② ③ ④
65. ① ② ③ ④
66. ① ② ③ ④
67. ① ② ③ ④
68. ① ② ③ ④
69. ① ② ③ ④
70. ① ② ③ ④
71. ① ② ③ ④
72. ① ② ③ ④
73. ① ② ③ ④
74. ① ② ③ ④
75. ① ② ③ ④
76. ① ② ③ ④
77. ① ② ③ ④
78. ① ② ③ ④
79. ① ② ③ ④
80. ① ② ③ ④
81. ① ② ③ ④
82. ① ② ③ ④
83. ① ② ③ ④
84. ① ② ③ ④
85. ① ② ③ ④
86. ① ② ③ ④
87. ① ② ③ ④
88. ① ② ③ ④
89. ① ② ③ ④
90. ① ②
91. ① ② ③ ④
92. ① ② ③ ④
93. ① ② ③ ④
94. ① ② ③ ④
95. ① ② ③ ④
96. ① ② ③ ④
97. ① ② ③ ④
98. ① ② ③ ④
99. ① ② ③ ④
100. ① ② ③ ④

Name ______________________

Exam Questions for CPT and HCPCS

Directions: Use the appropriate coding manual to determine the correct choice for each situation.

1. To report ambulance services for a Medicare patient ordered by a physician, use modifier:

   ① -QM

   ② -QN

   ③ -RC

   ④ -RT

2. A patient underwent simple incision and drainage of an abscess on his thigh. The wound was packed with iodoform gauze (approximately 2 x 2). Select the correct codes for the procedure and the gauze.

   ① 10060 + A6220

   ② 10060 + A6222

   ③ 10061 + A6222

   ④ 10061 + A6223

3. HCPCS Level II codes are four-position alphanumeric codes used to represent items not represented in Level I (CPT) codes.

   ① True

   ② False

4. A patient is to undergo an IVP but has a severe reaction to the contrast material and the IVP procedure is discontinued. Which modifier is used to describe this situation?

   ① -22

   ② -52

   ③ -53

   ④ -56

5. A patient was seen in the urgent care center with signs and symptoms of dehydration. She was observed for 8 hours while receiving IV normal saline infusion, 1000 cc. Select the correct HCPCS code for the infusion.

   ① J7030

   ② J7040

   ③ J7050

   ④ J7120

6. The L group of codes represents which procedures/products?

   ① pathology and laboratory

   ② drugs and enterals

   ③ orthotics and prosthetics

   ④ speech and language services

7. In CPT coding, the history, examination, and medical decision making are considered the key components in selecting the level of E/M services.

   ① True

   ② False

8. If a patient has trigger thumb release performed on the right, which modifier is used for the anatomic location?

   ① -F4

   ② -F5

   ③ -F9

   ④ -FA

9. A nursing facility patient developed multiple decubitus ulcers after a hospital stay. Her physician readmitted her to the nursing facility did a detailed exam, developed a new plan of care, and ordered an air fluidized bed for treatment. Select the correct E/M and HCPCS codes.

   ① 99304 + E0193

   ② 99304 + E0194

   ③ 99305 + E0193

   ④ 99305 + E0194

10. The use of HCPCS codes is mandatory on all Medicare and Medicaid claims submitted for payment for services of allied health care professionals.

   ① True

   ② False

11. A patient was seen in consultation for possible surgery. The surgeon schedules the procedure for the following day. Which modifier would you choose to indicate the decision for surgery?

   ① -54

   ② -55

   ③ -56

   ④ -57

12. Select the correct HCPCS code for an insertion tray without drainage bag or catheter.

   ① A4310

   ② A4311

   ③ A4312

   ④ A4313

13. Select the correct HCPCS code for surgical stockings, below-knee length.

   ① A4490

   ② A4495

   ③ A4500

   ④ A4510

14. In CPT coding, the definition of outpatient services would be those provided to a person who only stays in the hospital overnight.

   ① True

   ② False

15. A patient has incision and drainage of an abscess involving the left fourth toe. Identify the correct modifier.

   ① -T2

   ② -T3

   ③ -T6

   ④ -T8

16. The patient was seen in the office for a facial chemical peel, epidermal only.

   ① 15780

   ② 15786

   ③ 15788

   ④ 15789

17. K codes in HCPCS represent the official codes for durable medical equipment.

   ① True

   ② False

18. The patient was seen in the emergency department for acute shortness of breath. During his observation in the emergency department, multiple arterial blood gas testing was performed to monitor his improvement. Which modifier would you choose to accurately code the multiple ABGs?

   ① -51

   ② -90

   ③ -91

   ④ -99

19. Select the correct HCPCS code for a tourniquet used by a dialysis patient.

① A4911

② A4913

③ A4918

④ A4929

20. Select the correct HCPCS code for a pair of aluminum underarm crutches.

① E0110

② E0112

③ E0114

④ E0116

21. Physical status modifiers in CPT are used to distinguish the varying levels of complexity of surgical services provided.

① True

② False

22. A Medicare patient received a wheelchair two months ago, but the beneficiary has not decided whether to purchase or rent. Which HCPCS modifier would you use?

① -BO

② -BP

③ -BR

④ -BU

23. A teenage patient, new to the practice, was seen for signs and symptoms of tonsillitis and pharyngitis. She was given an injection of azithromycin for her acute symptoms. Select the correct E/M code and the HCPCS code.

① 99201 + J0456

② 99201 + J0530

③ 99202 + J0456

④ 99202 + J0530

24. It is acceptable to code HCPCS from index entries only.

① True

② False

25. A patient was seen by her family doctor for a routine physical exam. During the exam, the patient was noted to have high blood pressure. The physician discussed the new finding with the patient, and the patient disclosed she has been under a great deal of stress due to the demands of her work and impending divorce. The high blood pressure was deemed stress-related and the physician and the patient discussed stress-reduction techniques. As a result of the extended discussion with the patient, the visit was prolonged beyond the normally expected length for a routine physical exam. Which CPT modifier would you use to document the additional time spent with the patient?

① -21

② -22

③ -24

④ -25

26. Select the correct HCPCS code for a surgically implanted electrical osteogenesis stimulator.

① E0748

② E0749

③ E0760

④ E0761

27. Select the correct HCPCS code to report a patient receiving an injection of amphotericin B, 50 mg.

① J0285

② J0287 q = 5

③ J0288 q = 5

④ J0289 q = 5

28. The general definition of the CPT surgical package includes the patient's preoperative evaluation on the day of the procedure, the surgical procedure and its usual components, and the patient's uncomplicated follow-up care.

① True

② False

29. The patient had a skin tag removed from her upper left eyelid. Which HCPCS modifier describes this location?

① -El

② -E2

③ -E3

④ -E4

30. An infant born with clubfoot on the right was seen in the pediatric orthopedic clinic as a new patient. The physician conducted a problem-focused history and examination and prescribed a clubfoot wedge for the patient. Select the correct codes for the visit and the wedge.

① 99201 + L3201-RT

② 99201 + L3380-RT

③ 99212 + L3201-RT

④ 99212 + L3380-RT

31. The HCPCS route of administration abbreviation "IT" means the patient is receiving the drug intrathecally.

① True

② False

32. The patient was seen in the office for exercise stress testing. When the physician was placing the EKG leads, she noticed a suspicious mole on the patient's chest and excised the lesion. What CPT modifier would you use to indicate the additional procedure performed during this visit?

① -50

② -51

③ -52

④ -53

33. A patient was seen in the office for acute hives. The doctor gave her a 25 mg. injection of hydroxyzine. Select the correct HCPCS code.

① J3400

② J3410

③ J3470

④ J3485

34. Select the correct HCPCS code for an orthopedic shoe insole made of felt and covered with leather.

① L3520

② L3540

③ L3570

④ L3590

35. To measure and code the removal of a lesion using CPT guidelines, the lesion size must be expressed in inches.

① True

② False

36. If a patient is prescribed oxygen therapy at 0.5 liters per minute, which HCPCS modifier describes this flow rate?

① -QE

② -QF

③ -QG

④ -QH

37. An established patient was seen in the office because of difficulty toileting after hip replacement surgery. The physician examined the patient and sent her home with a stationary commode chair with fixed arms to use during her recovery period. Select the appropriate codes.

① 99211 + E0163

② 99211 + E0165

③ 99212 + E0163

④ 99212 + E0165

38. All HCPCS codes and descriptions are updated monthly by CMS.

① True

② False

39. Which CPT modifier would you choose to indicate a patient received a service or procedure that was less than originally intended?

① -22

② -32

③ -51

④ -52

40. Select the correct HCPCS code that describes the reduction of an ocular prosthesis.

① V2623

② V2625

③ V2626

④ V2629

41. A patient was given an intramuscular injection of 2 mg. of Haldol in the physician's office. Select the correct HCPCS code.

① J1630

② J1631

③ J3410

④ J3470

42. When coding bilateral procedures in CPT, you must always include the code 09950.

① True

② False

43. The mobile x-ray service came to the nursing facility to x-ray Mrs. Jones for possible hip fracture. The x-ray will be interpreted tomorrow by the radiologist. Which HCPCS modifier would you use for today's service?

① -TA

② -TC

③ -TD

④ -TE

44. A Medicare patient with diabetes saw the doctor for routine foot care: the trimming of three calluses and debridement of all 10 toenails.

① 11056 + 11719

② 11056 + 11721

③ 11057 + 11720

④ S0390

45. Laboratory services in HCPCS are listed in the P codes grouping.

① True

② False

46. Which CPT modifier would you use to indicate that an outside laboratory was used to process a patient's specimen?

① -56

② -90

③ -91

④ -99

47. Select the correct HCPCS code for a patient receiving nonemergency minibus transportation in a mountain area.

① A0080

② A0110

③ A0120

④ A0160

48. Many radiology procedures include two parts: a technical component and a professional component.

① True

② False

49. The patient has used his wheelchair for nearly four years. Due to wear, he now needs a replacement for the right footrest. Which HCPCS modifier is used to indicate this replacement?

① -RC

② -RP

③ -RR

④ -RT

50. A patient was referred to the office of a wound care specialist for consultation regarding his nonhealing surgical wound. The physician spent approximately 30 minutes with the patient and sent him home on topical hyperbaric oxygen chamber therapy for wound healing. Select the correct codes.

① 99241 + A4575

② 99242 + A4575

③ 99251 + A4575

④ 99252 + A4575

51. Drugs listed in HCPCS are identified by both brand and generic names.

① True

② False

52. A patient underwent emergency cholecystectomy six days after having a lung biopsy. The same surgeon performed both procedures. Which CPT modifier is used on the second surgery to indicate this type of situation?

① -58

② -59

③ -78

④ -79

53. Which of the following HCPCS code groups are listed for use only on a temporary basis?

① G, J, Q

② G, K, Q

③ J, K, Q

④ K, P, Q

54. A patient was seen for insertion of a temporary indwelling Foley urinary catheter. Select the correct codes.

① 51701 + A4314

② 51701 + A4338

③ 51702 + A4338

④ 51703 + A4328

55. According to CPT coding guidelines, a pathology consultation includes a medical interpretive report.

① True

② False

56. Dr. Wilkins amputated a patient's right lower extremity (BKA). His staff PA was the assistant during the procedure. Which HCPCS modifier would you choose to indicate the PA's role in this procedure?

① -AD

② -AM

③ -AS

④ -AT

57. Patient was seen by the nurse for a routine visit in the multiple sclerosis clinic. The patient received an injection of beta-1a interferon, 33 mcg., by the nurse in the clinic. Select the appropriate codes.

① 99211 + J1825

② 99211 + J9212 q=33

③ 99212 + J1825

④ 99212 + J9214

58. HCPCS ambulance modifiers always include one alpha character and one numeric character.

① True

② False

59. If a patient suddenly refuses to have surgery performed after being prepped for the procedure, which CPT modifier would you use to indicate the change in plans?

① -52

② -53

③ -56

④ none of the above

60. Select the correct HCPCS code for a drainable rubber ostomy pouch with a faceplate attached.

① A4375

② A4376

③ A4377

④ A4378

61. Select the correct HCPCS code for replacement handgrip for a cane that the patient owns.

① A4635

② A4636

③ A4637

④ A4640

62. In CPT coding, when the patient receives an immune globulin product, you must also include an administration code as appropriate.

① True

② False

63. An ambulance was called to come to the aid of a choking patient; however, the patient expired before the ambulance arrived on the scene. Which HCPCS modifier would you use to document this circumstance?

① -QK

② -QL

③ -QM

④ -QP

64. Patient underwent unattended sleep study with monitoring of oxygen saturation. The patient was not able to sleep adequately throughout the study and therefore the study was equivocal. The patient was provided with a recording apnea monitor for home use. Select the appropriate codes.

① 95806 + E0618

② 95806 + E0619

③ 95807 + E0618

④ 95807 + E0619

65. The two levels of national HCPCS codes can be applied to both inpatients and outpatients.

① True

② False

66. Which CPT modifier is used to indicate a repeat procedure performed by a different physician?

① -58

② -76

③ -77

④ -78

67. Select the correct HCPCS code for a hydrogel dressing with an adhesive border used to cover a wound, measuring 24 square inches.

① A6242

② A6243

③ A6246

④ A6248

68. Select the correct HCPCS code for home mix parenteral nutritional additives, to include electrolytes.

① B4197

② B4199

③ B4216

④ B4220

69. When coding in CPT, no distinction is made between new and established patients in the emergency department.

① True

② False

70. The patient was seen in the contraceptive clinic two weeks after delivery of her child. She was fitted with a copper intrauterine device. Select the codes for the fitting and the device.

① 58300 + J7303

② 58300 + J7300

③ 58301 + J7303

④ 58301 + J7300

71. Select the correct HCPCS code for a brake attachment for wheeled walker.

① E0143

② E0147

③ E0155

④ E0159

72. Select the correct HCPCS code for a patient admitted as an inpatient to a residential addiction program for acute alcohol detoxification.

① H0009

② H0011

③ H0012

④ H0013

73. A patient was fitted with a 2-lead TENS unit for pain control after suffering a fractured radius. Select appropriate codes.

① 64550 + E0720

② 64550 + E0730

③ 64575 + E0720

④ 64575 + E0730

74. Select the correct HCPCS code for an injection of methylprednisolone acetate, 40 mg.

① J1020 q = 2

② J1030

③ J1040

④ J1051

75. The patient came to the office to have a B12 level analysis and to receive her weekly B12 shot. Select the correct codes.

① 82607 + J3420

② 82607 + J3430

③ 82608 + J3420

④ 82608 + J3430

76. Select the HCPCS code that correctly identifies a unit of leukocyte-reduced platelets.

① P9019

② P9020

③ P9031

④ P9034

77. Select the correct HCPCS code for 1 mg. of inhaled dexamethasone in concentrated form.

① J1094

② J1100

③ J7637

④ J7638

78. A patient who is status post left-sided CVA was seen for weight loss and other symptoms indicative of dysphagia. She received dysphagia screening and her first treatment for the swallowing dysfunction. Select the correct codes.

① 92526 + V5362

② 92526 + V5364

③ 92610 + V5362

④ 92610 + V5364

79. Select the correct HCPCS code for a non-heated humidifier used with a positive airway pressure device.

① A7039

② E0550

③ E0560

④ E0561

80. The physician spent 30 minutes with the patient and family to discuss discharge plans on the day of discharge, as well as the patient's immediate at-home care. The patient had undergone his second below-knee amputation, and was given a transfer board for use at home. Select the codes for the discharge visit and the transfer board.

① 99238 + E0705

② 99238 + E1035

③ 99239 + E0705

④ 99239 + El035

81. Select the correct HCPCS code that reflects the supply of one vial of technetium Tc 99m disofenin.

① A9500

② A9502

③ A9510

④ A9536

82. Identify the HCPCS code that describes a full-leg, segmental pneumatic appliance with compressor.

① E0650

② E0660

③ E0667

④ E0671

83. Select the HCPCS code for a 50 mg. intravenous infusion of cisplatin in the physician's office.

① J0743

② J0770

③ J9060

④ J9062

84. To report the services of a CRNA directed by the anesthesiologist for the fifth procedure supervised by that physician, use modifier:

① -QS

② -QX

③ -QY

④ -QZ

85. To report the services of the physician in question 84, use modifier:

① -AA

② -AD

③ -QK

④ -QY

86. As part of the preschool program, the 4-year-old boy had a topical fluoride application.

① D1120

② D1203

③ D1204

④ D1206

87. A patient was fitted with a custom-made compression burn garment for severe burns of the chest and upper back.

① A6501

② A6509

③ A6510

④ A6511

88. The patient with a fractured femur and tibia had a trapeze and grab bar attached to a hospital bed in his home.

① E0910

② E0920

③ E0940

④ E0941

89. Five patients participated in the group psychotherapy session and received educational materials.

① 90806 + 99071

② 90846 + 99070

③ 90853 + 99071

④ 90901 + 99070

90. A 68-year-old male received a drainable ostomy pouch with an attached barrier.

① A5051

② A5054

③ A5061

④ A5071

91. The patient got a replacement for a lost gas permeable bifocal contact lens.

① V2430

② V2502

③ V2512

④ V2522

92. The codes in HCPCS that should not be reported to Medicare are the ones that begin with the letters:

① B, E, H, S

② D, G, H, T

③ D, H, S, T

④ H, K, S, T

93. A defined formula (100 calories to a unit) to meet a special metabolic need when administered through a feeding tube is reported with code:

① B4150

② B4152

③ B4153

④ B4154

94. Dr. Johnson serves a large rural area and some patients request their E/M services via the Internet. These documented encounters would be reported with code:

① 99056

② 99347

③ 99441

④ 99444

95. The infant with a left club foot was treated by manipulation and a short leg cast.

① 29405-LT

② 29425-LT

③ 29450-LT

④ 29799-LT

96. Mrs. Johnson was given a half-leg nonsegmental pneumatic appliance to use at home with her pneumatic compressor.

① E0655

② E0660

③ E0666

④ E0669

97. A shoe store specializing in diabetic shoes supplied the patient with a pair that had a metatarsal bar.

① A5500 q = 2

② A5503 q = 2

③ A5504 q = 2

④ A5505 q = 2

98. Following his hospitalization, the patient went home with cervical traction equipment that fit over a door.

① E0840

② E0850

③ E0860

④ E0870

99. The patient was authorized to receive a new 12 volt battery charger.

① L7360

② L7362

③ L7364

④ L7366

100. The patient received 1 g. of liquid immune globulin intravenously from the nurse in his doctor's office.

① 90281 + J1480

② 90281 + J1510

③ 90471 + J1510

④ 90765 + J1568 q=2

Name ____________________________

Answers to Exam Questions: CPT and HCPCS

1. ① ② ③ ④	26. ① ② ③ ④	51. ① ②	76. ① ② ③ ④
2. ① ② ③ ④	27. ① ② ③ ④	52. ① ② ③ ④	77. ① ② ③ ④
3. ① ②	28. ① ②	53. ① ② ③ ④	78. ① ② ③ ④
4. ① ② ③ ④	29. ① ② ③ ④	54. ① ② ③ ④	79. ① ② ③ ④
5. ① ② ③ ④	30. ① ② ③ ④	55. ① ②	80. ① ② ③ ④
6. ① ② ③ ④	31. ① ②	56. ① ② ③ ④	81. ① ② ③ ④
7. ① ②	32. ① ② ③ ④	57. ① ② ③ ④	82. ① ② ③ ④
8. ① ② ③ ④	33. ① ② ③ ④	58. ① ②	83. ① ② ③ ④
9. ① ② ③ ④	34. ① ② ③ ④	59. ① ② ③ ④	84. ① ② ③ ④
10. ① ②	35. ① ②	60. ① ② ③ ④	85. ① ② ③ ④
11. ① ② ③ ④	36. ① ② ③ ④	61. ① ② ③ ④	86. ① ② ③ ④
12. ① ② ③ ④	37. ① ② ③ ④	62. ① ②	87. ① ② ③ ④
13. ① ② ③ ④	38. ① ②	63. ① ② ③ ④	88. ① ② ③ ④
14. ① ②	39. ① ② ③ ④	64. ① ② ③ ④	89. ① ② ③ ④
15. ① ② ③ ④	40. ① ② ③ ④	65. ① ②	90. ① ② ③ ④
16. ① ② ③ ④	41. ① ② ③ ④	66. ① ② ③ ④	91. ① ② ③ ④
17. ① ②	42. ① ②	67. ① ② ③ ④	92. ① ② ③ ④
18. ① ② ③ ④	43. ① ② ③ ④	68. ① ② ③ ④	93. ① ② ③ ④
19. ① ② ③ ④	44. ① ② ③ ④	69. ① ②	94. ① ② ③ ④
20. ① ② ③ ④	45. ① ②	70. ① ② ③ ④	95. ① ② ③ ④
21. ① ②	46. ① ② ③ ④	71. ① ② ③ ④	96. ① ② ③ ④
22. ① ② ③ ④	47. ① ② ③ ④	72. ① ② ③ ④	97. ① ② ③ ④
23. ① ② ③ ④	48. ① ②	73. ① ② ③ ④	98. ① ② ③ ④
24. ① ②	49. ① ② ③ ④	74. ① ② ③ ④	99. ① ② ③ ④
25. ① ② ③ ④	50. ① ② ③ ④	75. ① ② ③ ④	100. ① ② ③ ④

Name ________________________

Exam Questions for ICD-9-CM

Directions: Use the appropriate coding manual to determine the correct choice for each situation.

1. A patient seen in the office today has known Graves' disease, now with signs and symptoms of a thyroid storm.

① 242.01

② 242.20

③ 242.90

④ 242.91

2. Three-year-old patient was brought in by her mother because of fever, fussiness, and tugging at the right ear. Otoscopy confirmed acute infection, with erythema and pus of the canal.

① 380.10

② 381.00

③ 381.10

④ 382.00

3. Patient was seen because of pain and swelling of the right elbow. The joint does not appear to be unstable. Rule out fracture.

① 719.02

② 719.42 + 719.02

③ 812.20

④ 812.40

4. The patient took the Ampicillin as directed but returns today with urticaria and swelling, classic signs of allergic reaction.

① 708.0

② 708.0 + 995.20

③ 708.0 + 995.20 + E930.0

④ 708.0 + E930.0

5. Newly diagnosed asthma patient was counseled regarding asthma therapy and the correct use of a nebulizer.

① V65.2

② V65.40

③ V65.49

④ V65.8

6. Select the correct code for ulcerative impetigo caused by a superficial staph infection.

① 111.9

② 684

③ 686.00

④ 686.9

7. Patient was seen for evaluation of pilonidal cyst.

① 173.5

② 685.0

③ 685.1

④ 686.00

8. Patient came to the office for examination of a penile lesion; physician determined it is a classic plaque of Peyronie's disease.

① 607.85

② 607.89

③ 608.89

④ 608.9

9. Patient was seen for annual gynecological exam including Pap smear.

① V70.0

② V70.9

③ V72.31

④ V76.2

10. Counseling regarding contraceptive use; patient received Norplant contraceptive 1 month ago.

① V25.09

② V25.40

③ V25.43

④ V65.40

11. Patient fell while snowboarding, suffering a dislocation of the left shoulder.

① 831.0

② 831.00 + E885.4

③ 831.09

④ 831.19 + E885.4

12. Select the correct code for a bilateral, non-strangulated inguinal hernia.

① 550.10

② 550.90

③ 550.92

④ 550.93

13. Patient was seen for vaginal spotting in her twenty-first week of pregnancy.

① 623.8

② 640.03

③ 640.93

④ 649.53

14. A 35-year-old female was seen in the office today for evaluation of a breast lump.

① 610.1

② 611.0

③ 611.2

④ 611.72

15. A 16-year-old male was seen in the clinic for severe sore throat, redness, cough, and erythema. Rapid strep test was positive.

① 034

② 034.0

③ 462 + 034.0

④ 463

16. Select the correct code for personal history of cervical carcinoma.

① 180.9

② 233.1

③ V10.40

④ V10.41

17. Patient was seen for continuing treatment of post-traumatic stress disorder.

① 309.0

② 309.81

③ 309.83

④ 309.9

18. Patient was diagnosed with bulimia.

① 307.50

② 307.51

③ 783.0

④ 783.6

19. Patient complains of diarrhea, abdominal cramping, and bloody stools. Rule out ulcerative colitis.

① 556.9

② 556.9 + 578.1 + 787.91

③ 578.1 + 787.91 + 789.00

④ 787.91

20. Child was seen for erythema and puncture wounds of the right forearm due to cat bite.

① 880.03

② 881.00

③ 881.00 + E906.3

④ E906.3

21. Patient came to the office to discuss treatment options for new diagnosis of malignant melanoma of the forehead.

① 172.0

② 172.3

③ 172.8

④ 172.9

22. Infant was brought in for evaluation of skin tags of the outer ear/earlobe.

① 744.1

② 744.29

③ 757.39

④ 757.8

23. Patient's daughter brought her father in for follow-up of progressive Alzheimer's dementia.

① 294.10

② 294.8

③ 331.0

④ 331.0 + 294.10

24. Child was brought into the office for evaluation and examination after swallowing a dime.

① 933.0

② 934.8

③ 935.2

④ 938

25. Vacationing patient was seen in the urgent care clinic for second-degree sunburn of both shoulder areas.

① 692.74

② 692.76

③ 692.82

④ 692.89

26. Select the correct code for Lyme disease.

① 088.0

② 088.81

③ 088.89

④ 088.9

27. Patient came into the office seeking treatment for fungal toenail infection.

① 110.1

② 110.8

③ 681.11

④ 681.9

28. Patient was seen in the office today requesting medications to assist with alcohol withdrawal.

① 291.0

② 291.4

③ 291.81

④ 291.89

29. Patient was seen for follow-up of replantation of amputated long finger.

① 883.0

② 884.0

③ 886.0

④ 886.1

30. A 6-year-old patient was brought in for additional testing for color blindness.

① 368.55

② 368.59

③ 368.60

④ 368.8

31. Patient was evaluated for somnolence relating to reactive hypoglycemia.

① 251.1

② 251.1 + 780.09

③ 251.2 + 780.02

④ 251.2 + 780.09

32. Select the correct code(s) for malignant hypertensive heart disease with renal failure.

① 401.0 + 593.9

② 403.90

③ 404.02

④ 405.01

33. Patient was seen for preoperative cardiovascular evaluation prior to undergoing cholecystectomy.

① V72.81

② V72.83

③ V72.85

④ V72.9

34. Patient was seen in follow-up for boxer's fracture of the right extremity.

① 814.00

② 815.00

③ 815.09

④ 815.10

35. Select the correct code(s) for cellulitis of the colostomy site.

① 569.60

② 569.61 + 682.2

③ 682.2 + 041.10

④ 998.59

36. Select the correct code for congenital bowleggedness.

① 736.42

② 736.5

③ 754.40

④ 754.44

37. Patient was seen by the gastroenterologist for evaluation of prolapsed internal hemorrhoids and anal fissure.

① 455.1 + 565.0

② 455.2 + 565.0

③ 455.5 + 565.1

④ 455.8 + 565.0

38. Patient was seen in the office for severe vertigo and loss of hearing. The patient was diagnosed with viral labyrinthitis.

① 386.19

② 386.30

③ 386.35

④ 780.4

39. Select the correct code(s) for idiopathic scoliosis with backache.

① 724.5

② 737.30

③ 737.30 + 724.5

④ 737.43

40. Patient was evaluated for varicose veins with stasis dermatitis of the left lower extremity.

① 447.2

② 451.0

③ 453.8

④ 454.11

41. Twenty-year-old patient was seen for continuing evaluation of Turner's syndrome.

① 752.7

② 758.6

③ 758.7

④ 758.89

42. Patient was seen with complaints of melena and anemia. Patient has strong family history of stomach cancer.

① 578.1 + 280.0 + V10.04

② 578.1 + 280.0 + V16.0

③ 578.9 + 280.0 + V16.0

④ V16.0

43. Select the correct codes for diabetic cataracts.

① 250.50 + 366.41

② 250.50 + 366.9

③ 250.51 + 366.41

④ 250.51 + 366.09

44. Patient was seen in follow-up for right bundle branch block with incomplete left bundle branch block.

① 426.4 + 426.3

② 426.51

③ 426.53

④ 426.54

45. The patient is status post PTCA, in for a one-week follow-up visit.

① V45.81

② V45.82

③ V67.00

④ V67.9

46. Patient was seen for complaints of fatigue and was noted to have diffuse adenopathy. Rule out leukemia.

① 208.00

② 208.80

③ 785.6 + 208.00

④ 785.6 + 780.79

47. Patient's chief complaint is losing her sense of smell after a bout of the flu.

① 349.9

② 781.1

③ 782.0

④ 799.2

48. Patient was seen for treatment of situational depression due to impending divorce.

① 308.3

② 309.0

③ 309.1

④ 309.24

49. Select the correct code for acquired trigger finger.

① 727.03

② 727.09

③ 756.89

④ 756.9

50. Select the correct code for rupture of the Achilles tendon.

① 726.71

② 727.50

③ 727.60

④ 727.67

51. Patient was seen for vaginal bleeding; placenta previa was detected. Patient is in early second trimester of pregnancy.

① 640.03

② 641.03

③ 641.10

④ 641.13

52. Select the correct code for narcolepsy.

① 301.81

② 307.45

③ 347.00

④ 780.50

53. Patient had episodes of "zoning out" and, after extensive observation and testing, was diagnosed with absence seizures.

① 345.00

② 345.01

③ 345.10

④ 345.40

54. Child was found to have a severe allergy to dog hair.

① 477.0

② 477.2

③ 477.9

④ 478.1

55. Patient was seen for treatment of frostbite of the toes.

① 991.2

② 991.3

③ 991.5

④ 991.6

56. Patient received an accidental, self-inflicted laceration of the palm of his hand while using a kitchen knife.

① 880.03 + E920.3

② 882.0 + E920.3

③ 882.0 + E920.8

④ 883.0 + E920.3

57. Patient was seen in consultation for several episodes of hydrocodone addiction.

① 304.02

② 304.62

③ 304.72

④ 305.42

58. Patient visiting from out of state was treated for headache, nausea, and vomiting. The patient was diagnosed with altitude sickness.

① 784.0

② 787.01

③ 993.2

④ E902.0

59. Select the correct code for acute viral conjunctivitis.

① 032.81

② 077.4

③ 077.99

④ 372.03

60. Select the correct codes for accidental poisoning with whiskey.

① 980.0 + E860.0

② 980.0 + E860.1

③ 980.9 + E860.2

④ 980.9 + E860.0

61. Patient returns to the office for ongoing evaluation of dysphasia. He suffered a cerebrovascular accident six months ago.

① 438.12

② 438.19

③ 784.49

④ 784.5

62. Select the correct codes for metastatic carcinoma of the liver with unknown primary.

① 155.0 + 239.0

② 197.7 + 199.1

③ 197.7 + 155.0

④ 197.7 + 239.0

63. The patient was seen in the office for complaints of halitosis.

① 783.9

② 784.49

③ 784.99

④ 786.3

64. Select the correct code for central corneal ulcer probably due to improper contact lens use and care.

① 370.00

② 370.03

③ 370.33

④ 370.49

65. The patient was seen by the orthopedic physician regarding carpal tunnel syndrome.

① 354.0

② 354.00

③ 354.8

④ 354.9

66. The patient suffered a severe burn over one year ago and is being evaluated for continued neuropathy of the left thigh secondary to the burn.

① 353.6 + 906.8

② 355.71 + 906.7

③ 355.8 + 906.7

④ 355.8 + 906.8

67. Patient was seen in the office for pain due to phantom limb syndrome.

① 353.4

② 353.6

③ 353.8

④ 353.9

68. Select the correct code for arteriovenous malformation of the right lower extremity requiring surgical treatment.

① 747.49

② 747.60

③ 747.64

④ 757.9

69. Infant was seen in the office today for follow-up of Tetrology of Fallot.

① 745.10

② 745.2

③ 746.09

④ 746.4

70. Patient is being treated in the hospital for severe mitral regurgitation.

① 394.9

② 396.0

③ 424.0

④ 424.1

71. Patient was treated for a laceration and puncture wound of the right nostril; fish hook accidentally embedded in nostril.

① 873.20 + E920.8

② 873.22 + E920.8

③ 873.29 + E920.9

④ 873.39 + E920.8

72. Select the correct code for chronic familial pemphigus.

① 694.4

② 694.60

③ 757.39

④ 785.4

73. Patient returns to the office for physical therapy to regain strength in his back after a thoracic muscle strain at work.

① 847.1 + V57.1

② 847.9 + V57.1

③ V57.1 + 847.1

④ V57.89 + 847.1

74. Select the correct code for temporomandibular joint syndrome (TMJ).

① 524.4

② 524.60

③ 524.69

④ 524.9

75. Patient was seen for evaluation and treatment of neurogenic bladder.

① 596.4

② 596.53

③ 596.54

④ 596.8

76. Patient came to the office with urinary symptoms. On digital exam, the patient was found to have a multinodular prostate gland.

① 600.00

② 600.10

③ 600.3

④ 600.91

77. The patient was seen today for weekly chemotherapy infusion; recent diagnosis of primary carcinoma of the descending colon.

① V58.11 + 153.2

② V58.11 + 235.2

③ V66.2 + 153.2

④ V66.2 + 235.2

78. Patient is being seen for acute reactive depression due to recent diagnosis of pancreatic cancer.

① 289.9 + 239.0

② 300.4 + 157.1

③ 300.4 + 157.9

④ 300.4 + 239.0

79. Select the correct code for acute sinusitis, in conjunction with influenza.

① 461.9

② 473.8

③ 473.9 + 487.1

④ 487.1 + 461.9

80. The patient was assaulted and suffered a periorbital hematoma, nasal bone fracture, and chipped tooth.

① 921.2 + 802.0 + 873.63 + E960.0

② 921.2 + 802.0 + 873.79 + E960.0

③ 921.3 + 802.0 + 873.63 + E960.0

④ 921.9 + 802.0 + 873.79 + E960.0

81. Select the correct code(s) for a hiatal hernia with obstruction.

① 552.3

② 552.9

③ 553.8

④ 750.6

82. Patient complains of insomnia.

① 307.42

② 307.49

③ 780.51

④ 780.52

83. Patient is evaluated for sudden total blindness of the right eye; left eye was not affected.

① 368.60

② 369.60

③ 369.63

④ 369.64

84. Select the correct code for cardiac asthma.

① 428.1

② 428.22

③ 493.20

④ 493.90

85. Adult male was diagnosed with whooping cough due to parapertussis.

① 033.1

② 033.9

③ 306.1

④ 786.2

86. Patient was suffering from near-syncope episodes and was diagnosed with an electrolyte imbalance.

① 276.0

② 276.4

③ 276.50

④ 276.9

87. Patient is HIV positive and now has evidence of Kaposi lesions on the skin.

① 042

② 042 + 176.0

③ 757.33

④ 176.0 + V08

88. Female in her third trimester of pregnancy has obvious dependent edema.

① 643.80

② 646.10

③ 646.13

④ 646.20

89. The patient has been diagnosed with multiple sclerosis.

① 337.9

② 340

③ 341.8

④ 341.9

90. Select the correct code for a pathologic fracture of the distal radius.

① 733.10

② 733.12

③ 733.19

④ 813.42

91. The patient was seen today for arthritis related to a salmonella infection.

① 003.0

② 003.20

③ 003.23

④ 003.8

92. Female diagnosed with Darling's endocarditis.

① 115.00

② 115.03

③ 115.04

④ 115.09

93. The patient worked with talc for many years and is now diagnosed with pneumoconiosis.

① 500

② 502

③ 503

④ 505

94. A 17-year-old male has second degree burns of both ankles and feet caused by fireworks.

① 945.03 + E923.0

② 945.23 + E923.0

③ 945.29 + E923.0

④ 946.2 + E923.0

95. The patient will take an early retirement due to complications of post-polio syndrome.

① 045.12

② 045.90

③ 046.1

④ 138

96. An elderly woman is seen for multiple neuropathies following shingles.

① 053.10

② 053.13

③ 353.8

④ 356.4

97. The patient fell from his horse and was diagnosed with a C2 fracture and posterior cord syndrome.

① 806.00 + E828.2

② 806.04 + E828.2

③ 806.09 + E827.2

④ 805.12 + E827.2

98. A 78-year-old became comatose when given the insulin ordered for the patient in the next bed.

① 250.30

② 962.3

③ 995.23

④ 995.4

99. The patient was diagnosed with septicemia secondary to anthrax.

① 022.0

② 022.3

③ 022.8

④ 038.9

100. The patient received a laceration of the carotid artery while harvesting hay.

① 900.00 + E920.8

② 900.00 + E919.0

③ 900.01 + E919.8

④ 998.2 + E920.8

Name ____________________

Answers to Exam Questions: ICD–9–CM

1. ① ② ③ ④
2. ① ② ③ ④
3. ① ② ③ ④
4. ① ② ③ ④
5. ① ② ③ ④
6. ① ② ③ ④
7. ① ② ③ ④
8. ① ② ③ ④
9. ① ② ③ ④
10. ① ② ③ ④
11. ① ② ③ ④
12. ① ② ③ ④
13. ① ② ③ ④
14. ① ② ③ ④
15. ① ② ③ ④
16. ① ② ③ ④
17. ① ② ③ ④
18. ① ② ③ ④
19. ① ② ③ ④
20. ① ② ③ ④
21. ① ② ③ ④
22. ① ② ③ ④
23. ① ② ③ ④
24. ① ② ③ ④
25. ① ② ③ ④
26. ① ② ③ ④
27. ① ② ③ ④
28. ① ② ③ ④
29. ① ② ③ ④
30. ① ② ③ ④
31. ① ② ③ ④
32. ① ② ③ ④
33. ① ② ③ ④
34. ① ② ③ ④
35. ① ② ③ ④
36. ① ② ③ ④
37. ① ② ③ ④
38. ① ② ③ ④
39. ① ② ③ ④
40. ① ② ③ ④
41. ① ② ③ ④
42. ① ② ③ ④
43. ① ② ③ ④
44. ① ② ③ ④
45. ① ② ③ ④
46. ① ② ③ ④
47. ① ② ③ ④
48. ① ② ③ ④
49. ① ② ③ ④
50. ① ② ③ ④
51. ① ② ③ ④
52. ① ② ③ ④
53. ① ② ③ ④
54. ① ② ③ ④
55. ① ② ③ ④
56. ① ② ③ ④
57. ① ② ③ ④
58. ① ② ③ ④
59. ① ② ③ ④
60. ① ② ③ ④
61. ① ② ③ ④
62. ① ② ③ ④
63. ① ② ③ ④
64. ① ② ③ ④
65. ① ② ③ ④
66. ① ② ③ ④
67. ① ② ③ ④
68. ① ② ③ ④
69. ① ② ③ ④
70. ① ② ③ ④
71. ① ② ③ ④
72. ① ② ③ ④
73. ① ② ③ ④
74. ① ② ③ ④
75. ① ② ③ ④
76. ① ② ③ ④
77. ① ② ③ ④
78. ① ② ③ ④
79. ① ② ③ ④
80. ① ② ③ ④
81. ① ② ③ ④
82. ① ② ③ ④
83. ① ② ③ ④
84. ① ② ③ ④
85. ① ② ③ ④
86. ① ② ③ ④
87. ① ② ③ ④
88. ① ② ③ ④
89. ① ② ③ ④
90. ① ② ③ ④
91. ① ② ③ ④
92. ① ② ③ ④
93. ① ② ③ ④
94. ① ② ③ ④
95. ① ② ③ ④
96. ① ② ③ ④
97. ① ② ③ ④
98. ① ② ③ ④
99. ① ② ③ ④
100. ① ② ③ ④